# STROKING the MEDIA

## The Anchorman's Guide To Free Publicity

### by Brian Wilkes

With contributions by

## Mark Ress and Robert Yehling

ISBN-13: 978-1484112212
ISBN-10: 1484112210

# STROKING the MEDIA

## The Anchorman's Guide To Becoming Newsworthy and Getting Free Publicity You Couldn't BUY!

### *by Brian Wilkes*

## Contents

---

## Table of Contents

# Preface

PHINEAS T. BARNUM.

In modern American English, **advertising** is paid media exposure, and **publicity** is free media exposure. In other parts of the world, both are call publicity. We use it to mean **unpaid.**

American promoter **P.T. Barnum** reportedly once said "There's no such thing as bad publicity."

English writer **Oscar Wilde** observed "The only thing worse than being talked about is **not** being talked about."

Irish writer **Brendan Behan** said "There's no such thing as bad publicity, except your own obituary."

Our goal here is to get you the best possible free publicity - frequent mention in legitimate news stories. I write from the perspective of a former news director, anchor and talk show host who was on the receiving end of hundreds of news releases every week. Most of the "gurus" in this field haven't been there.

PS: There IS such a thing as bad publicity... and there are remedies!

# The Voracious News Beast

**In the past generation, the changes in mass media have increased the demand for fresh news content many times over. This works to your benefit!**

Once upon a time, most towns were lucky to have a weekly newspaper. The largest cities had daily newspapers, and some had both morning and evening newspapers. The world has changed!

In the late 1970s, the growth of all-news radio stations and superstations like WGN in Chicago and WTBS in Atlanta, its offspring Cable News Network and the legion of 24 hour news networks that followed, expanded the profession of journalism as news outlets competed for stories. Where a news team of professionals might spend the whole day to fill two or three half-hour newscasts or a single edition of a newspaper, and a **60 Minutes** crew might have the luxury of months to investigate and verify all aspects of a story, they now had to do that same volume of work two or three times each hour. The result was the creation of a News Beast, which voraciously devoured all of the news set before it, and hungrily demanded more. The proliferation of news outlets across the country meant hundreds of them, bottomless pits, demanding fresh content every hour. Think back to the carnivorous potted plant in *Little Shop of Horrors*, yelling "FEED ME!"

Once upon a time, professional journalists could afford to be very choosy when reviewing and evaluating potential news stories. Submitting a news release to a news outlet was certainly no guarantee that the story would go anywhere - except into the trash can. Today, as news outlets deal with smaller budgets and smaller staffs, journalists need all the friends they can get to keep them informed, to be their all eyes and ears in different parts of the region and in various diverse communities.

The purpose of this book is to help you to help your local and regional news media. If you follow the advice in this book, you will become their best friend, learn and understand their changing needs, and become a reliable source of **legitimate** news information. Once in awhile, the information you provide will also provide exposure for your own business, charity, organization, or similar venture.

There are many books and courses that teach you how to prepare and submit press releases using high-tech online service. **Stroking The Media** teaches you how to use the low-tech/high touch approach to become a news source upon whom the news media can rely on when something unexpected hits the news cycle.

# The True Brotherhood of Journalists

**Journalists strive to be public servants with high ethical standards, whose word will be accepted as truth. They know many will try to use them to spread lies.**

A century ago, the crime reporter risked his life to reveal corruption. The crusading investigative reporter revealed the truth about Twenties gangs and the growing Nazi menace to the victimized public. This made journalism in the first half of the 20th century an attractive career choice for idealistic young people.

While they signed up for the comic book fantasy at left, rubbing shoulders with Clark Kent and Brenda Starr, what they found was more the pre-cubicle newsroom.

To paraphrase Walter Lippman, founder of **New Republic** magazine, the average citizen hasn't the specialized education or available time to analyze complex issues. They depend on the news media to deliver and explain the world to them in bite-sized chunks - pre-digested, when possible. The news media is the town crier, watchdog, and analyst. The duty of the media was not only to report what various parties to an issue claimed, but to go a step further and tell us which parties were blatant deceiver or just plain wrong.

*Newsrooms of the **New Orleans Time-Picayune** in 1900 (center), and **New York Times** in 1942 (bottom). Each used the cutting edge technology of its day. Understanding both the prevailing siege mentality and frat house attitudes will help you deal with the media. (Note the woman at the center of the 1900 photo - journalism was one of the first venues to accept women, as long as they wrote under a man's by-line!*

Journalism in the second half of the 20<sup>th</sup> century was shaped by this idea of a higher calling, embodied in the team that CBS legend Edward R. Murrow assembled to cover Europe as World War 2 loomed. These were Mary Marvin Breckinridge (a woman who originally used a man's name), Cecil Brown, Winston Burdett, Charles Collingwood, William Downs, Thomas Grandin, Richard C. Hottelet, Larry LeSueur, Eric Sevareid, William L. Shirer, and Howard K. Smith. Most of the "Murrow Boys" would go on to become major correspondents and anchors themselves.

At a time when many Americans thought we should stay out of the new European war, or openly supported either Fascism or Communism, Murrow reported honestly on the human toll of the London Blitz, which eventually took 40,000 lives, and left many thousands orphaned and homeless. Londoners said goodbye to their neighbors before the blackout each evening with "good night and good luck," a wish that each would survive the night. After hearing Princess Elizabeth use it to close her radio broadcast, he adopted it as his trademark sign-off. Today, it sounds almost trite, but at the time, it was clear Murrow was warning Americans they the USA was also a target.

Murrow said, said "To be persuasive, we must be believable; to be believable, we must be credible; to be credible, we must be truthful." Whether they express it that way or not, today's journalists still believe that, and are more like to find rapport with you if believe the same, and conduct yourself accordingly.

Author **Tom Wolfe** once called the news establishment "the Genteel Beast," comparing it to a hypocritical self-censoring Victorian gentleman, fascinated with lurid things, yet wanting to appear above reproach. The Genteel Beast will drag you through shocking, sordid details, all under the guise of the public interest and the right to know.

While the pendulum has occasionally swung to "happy talk" news and hairspray overdose, the majority of those I worked with in the media believed they were performing a public service essential to the stability of the republic, and considered themselves public servants even though they worked for private corporations. This frequently caused stress between the outlet management and the news staff.

Journalism is the lowest-paid profession, and perhaps the only profession that does not require government licensing. At the same time, many if not most journalists believe that it's more of a calling than a job. They are called to it the way some are called to the priesthood, or the military, or emergency services work. If you're just in it for the money, it's a poor choice. Many journalists are barely paying the bills.

Often misunderstood and misperceived by the general public, serious journalists develop a feeling of isolation and even martyrdom, a siege mentality. They worry that people will take a "blame the messenger" attitude when they bring bad news. No matter what they report, somebody accuses them of partisanship.

As a result, they prefer to keep to others of their own type, and are always looking for a new ally. When it comes to news tips, they prefer to deal with another one of the "brotherhood." There's no secret handshake, but if you can learn to think like a journalist, you'll be able to better anticipate their needs.

# My Own Qualifications

I've worked in almost every field of journalism, and I've been the one who decided which news sources and releases could be trusted or used.

*With Walter Cronkite In Palm Beach, 1981*

Remember this rule: **Thou Shalt Not BORE!**   I won't bore you with the details of my life. I started writing and anchoring news while still in college for both the campus newspaper and radio station as the Watergate scandal was heating up. (I actually had brief access to one of the Watergate burglars before President Nixon resigned.)

If you watch the movie "All The President's Men,"  it will take you back to a day when reporting was done with telephones and shoe leather and sifting through mountains of paper notes. But it will also take you back to an America that briefly regarded journalists as self-sacrificing national heroes.

A few years later, I entered the field full time as a street reporter, anchor, and talk show host. Eventually, I was responsible for seven newscasts and two live talk shows daily. My next two jobs were as news director and anchor at stations on the Space Coast of Florida as the Space Shuttle program ramped up.

From there, I became part of a team that helped a station in West Palm Beach make the transition to an all-news and news/talk format, as the superior audio quality of FM drove nails into the coffin of AM music radio. I went next to a statewide news network, and then to New York where I was the token moderate at a progressive radio station. I've also worked for newspapers, national magazines, wire services, and syndicated television sports.

My news career spans almost 20 years, but the important points for you:
- I've worked in all media
- I've done almost every aspect of broadcast and print news media
- I was usually the one deciding which news releases to follow up, and which to trash.

So I'm qualified to tell you what is newsworthy, what will get your story tip used, and what will get it "spiked".

# The Era of Info-mercials, Info-tainment, and Pseudo-News

**The hard edges between news, entertainment, and advertisement have been blurred in recent years, so you must be clear on the difference before you attempt to pitch a story.**

When you buy **advertising**, either print or broadcast, it's pretty well assumed that you can say anything you like about your product or service as long as you don't make unlawful claims. For example, you can't claim that you've found a cure for an ailment unless your claims have been evaluated by the Food and Drug Administration. Whatever is contained in a paid ad is not verified or endorsed by the media outlet that runs it.

The **news** is another matter. Journalism is based on critical examination of all claims. When people read a news story, they rightly presume the facts have been checked and double-checked, the sources have been vetted and verified, and that unproven opinions have been removed or clearly labeled.

It's been known for generations that people are resistant to sales pitches and advertising. They are far less resistant or suspicious of genuine news, especially when that news is delivered by a trusted source.

As an anchor for two CBS affiliates, I was fortunate to spend some time with Walter Cronkite. One evening at dinner he turned to me and said, "You have to be able to look people right in the eye and tell them things they don't want to hear. The secret in this business of broadcast news is *credibility*." He paused. "If you can fake *that*, you've got it made."

The joke of course, is the Cronkite was called "the most trusted man in America." The secret there, he said, was not in convincing people of what he believed, but in finding out where they stood, determining the exact center of the ever-shifting ground of public opinion, and then standing there and owning that space as if he had been there all along.

Each news outlet, from the major global networks to the local weekly newspaper, tries to do the same thing within their target market.

*Invasion by Monsters from Mars*

An invasion from Mars changed the nature of news for the next 50 years. On October 30, 1938, an adaptation of the H. G. Wells novel *The War of the Worlds* was performed as a Halloween episode of the CBS Radio network, directed and narrated by Orson Welles. About the first 40 minutes of the production was a series of simulated news bulletins, gradually revealing to the listeners that an invasion by Martians was under in New Jersey, about halfway between New York and Philadelphia. The production ran without commercial break, as listeners would expect in a real emergency. Some of those who had not heard the disclaimer at the beginning or mid-point of the program thought it was live coverage of a genuine event. Although the broadcast has become part of American folklore, the incidents of invasion panic were few and isolated. But for our purpose, the deeper message is that the American people believed what they were told by professional journalists, or in this case, by their impostors.

Forty five years later, **Special Bulletin** used the same news bulletin format, this time in the guise of the fictitious RBS TV network, to portray a terrorist group's placement of a homemade nuclear weapon aboard a tugboat in the harbor of Charleston, South Carolina in order to blackmail the U.S. Government into disabling its nuclear weapons. Despite frequent disclaimers, some viewers became convinced the event was happening live.

In the wake of these and other incidents, media outlets strengthened the fence between news, advertising and entertainment with rules prohibiting the use of newscast formats for commercials. In print media, the standard practice is to separate the advertising content from the news content with a heavier border line than the one used to separate various news stories. The paid advertising is kept clearly separate.

In the 60's and 70's, NBC's **Today** show blurred the lines by having their newscasters also do commercial segments. It's been a hot issue among journalists not to blur the lines between the independent, objective news role and the promotional role of advertising. For that reason, many broadcast outlets don't use their news staff to produce commercials (other than promos for the station or newscasts themselves). When the audience sees or hears the newscaster say something, they should not have to wonder whether that personality is wearing his or her objective hat or promotional hat at this moment. Blurring of these roles leads to general distrust of the news department.

The Federal Communications Commission (FCC) established regulations in the 1950s and 1960s to govern and limit the commercial content of television. Infomercials proliferated after 1984 when those regulations were eliminated by the Reagan administration. **Infomercials** exploded in the mid-1990s with motivational, exercise and personal development products. Many of these aired on new cable outlets and independent stations which did not follow the same restrictions against imitation newscasts. An estimated $150 billion of consumer products are sold through infomercials each year in the US alone.

Infomercials are often made to closely resemble actual television programs. Some imitate talk shows and try to downplay the fact that the program is actually an advertisement.

The first infomercial (as we know it today) aired in 1982, when an entrepreneur marketed a hair growth treatment in a broadcast that imitated an investigative news report segment. *Robert Vaughan Discovers* copied the **ABC Nightline** format in a series of 30-minute infomercials that ran for 16 years.

**Pseudo news** is often aired on local television where it may take the form of a dramatic presentation of entertaining, sensationalized or celebrity-driven "tabloid" style stories. **Inside Edition**, **A Current Affair**, **Hard Copy** and others peaked in the Nineties.

In local television news, and on some cable channels, pseudo news is based on video news releases provided by advertisers, local companies, or affiliated entities within the station's corporate family.

On cable, pseudo news also comes in the form of comedic entertainment such as offered by **The Daily Show** and **The Colbert Report**. However, these are clearly labeled as satirical comedy programs. The scary thing is when they actually give a more accurate picture of world events and more hard-edged investigative reporting than the "professional" mainstream journalists.

The situation is even worse on the Internet, where anyone with basic skills can create an authentic-looking "news" site which is actually a collection of highly biased or unverified articles submitted by untrained and unvetted writers. The result is little better than a supermarket tabloid without the photos.

# Why A News Story is Worth FAR More Than Paid Advertising

**The public presumes news content to be objective, fair, balanced, and thoroughly researched, and accordingly they will lower the levels of skepticism they crank up for commercial messages.**

One of the moguls of US media was the late William Randolph Hearst. When a young minister named Billy Graham was beginning his career, Hearst ordered his editors to "Puff (promote) Graham," The evangelist appeared bewildered when describing how certain reporters had told him, "You've just been 'kissed' by William Randolph Hearst." Henry Luce, founder of *TIME, LIFE*, and *Fortune* magazines, followed suit. Luce had articles specifically written about Billy Graham, and put him on the cover of TIME magazine in 1954. Thus a bright, folksy, charismatic and photogenic preacher began the climb that would make him the best-known spokesman for Protestant Christianity.

While it's a long shot that you or your business will ever be "kissed" in a similarly grand manner, you can definitely get "stroked" - but you have to Stroke The Media first.

Here's the important point:

1. You can BUY advertising space and time, but many viewers will devalue it or tune it out because they know it's you promoting yourself.

2. You can be the SUBJECT of a news story, in which you are stroked by the media who (presumably) have checked and validated the facts.

3. You can be regularly CITED as an authority in one or more fields, in which you are KISSED by the media as someone they not only validate, but whom even **they** go to for information or validation.

Let's face it, if you're a small business or a start-up, you simply can't afford a large advertising schedule. You have to be creative in finding other ways to get your name and message in front of people.

If your business is a classic brick-and-mortar, most of your income will come from within a 30 mile radius. Even if you have a primarily online business that reaches out globally, as I do, you will find that news media within your 30-mile radius will be the ones most likely to do a story on you.

So here's the formula we'll follow, starting with your local market (10 - 30 mile radius):

1. Submit stories that are picked up by the **business** or **features** sections,
2. Submit stories that are picked up by the main **news** section,
3. Become a featured **columnist** or **editorialist**, (start with Letters to the Editor)
4. Become an **authority** the reporters seek out for comment on breaking news.

We will start by concentrating on the print media, simply because you can create scans of the result to use in future campaigns.

# Planning Your Self-Serving Publicity Campaign

Self-serving? Absolutely! You're setting off on a campaign to promote your own name, reputation, cause, and business. You are attempting to become a recognized authority, if not a household name. You can put a more altruistic spin on it for public consumption, if you like, but never lie to yourself. You are about to become an unabashed, aggressive, self-serving self-promoter. If you think there's something wrong in any of that, get over it now. The point of this game isn't exercise and good sportsmanship, it's about learning the rules, playing by the rules, and winning. If you can't get behind that concept, you should stop now and hire a professional publicist to do it all for you.

Still with me? Good.

## 1. Set Your Goals

We need to determine **what you want to accomplish** with your unpaid media campaign.
- Do you want to be perceived as someone who takes a serious civic interest in your community?
- Do you want to social-climb into the position of community leader?

- Do you want to make your name known to new prospects in the business community, or to the general public?
- Is your target market more likely to be business with annual sales of $500K and up, or the average dog owner?
- Are you more interested in establishing yourself, your brand, or your employer in the public consciousness?

The answers to questions like these will help you focus your campaign. You're not running for mayor or governor, but you **are** running for the title of expert in your field.

There will be days when you're in the news spotlight and you'll wonder why you ever agreed to an interview. Having clear goals at the outset will remind you, and may save you from too many wild goose chases.

As we mentioned earlier, media outlets are always on the hunt for new content. The mere fact that you appear on television or are interviewed by the news media will automatically position you as an expert in the minds of most people.

## 2. Research The News Media

Take the home court advantage! The media outlets most likely to use your feeds are those closest to you. They are always looking for a local angle to larger stories, and especially if you live outside of a major city, they are more likely to use you. I'll describe 'local' as within a 30-mile radius. Look at a map, draw a circle. That's where we'll research first.

With the Internet, it's a pretty simple matter to find every media outlet in your local ring. List them. Then find out which have their own news departments - today, many radio outlets "pipe in" a syndicated source.

## Media Directory Services

I'm not explaining a unique approach here. Many public relations companies have made a career of compiling directories of media outlets, automating submission processes, and including high-tech measurements. You can get into that game for as little as $1,500 per year, but expect to pay $3,000 - $6,000 per year for real impact.

- **Cision**         http://www.cision.com
- **Vocus**          http://www.vocus.com
- **Burrelle Luce**  http://www.burrelles.com.
- **Media Finder**   http://www.mediafinder.com
- **PR Web**         http://www.prweb.com
- **PR Newswire**    http://www.prnewswire.com

There are the "authority" submission sites that will be taken seriously and which may help in your release being picked up by Google News, one of the "big dogs" online. But there's still a very good chance your release will be lost and overlooked in the flood of thousands of releases submitted daily.

Or, you can learn the basics, do the research work and compile a customized directory yourself!

- **NewsLink**          http://www.newslink.org

**NewsLink** gives you the basic information and contacts for newspapers, radio and TV stations, organized by state and country. Find all print outlets within your 30-mile radius, and enter basic information into a document or spreadsheet. Many will even list their web sites, which is where we go for the next step.

I'm not saying that you shouldn't consider using some of the services above to help in your campaign (if you can afford them. But remember, these services are used by **hucksters** trying to **sell a product**. We're training you to become and **authority** offering to **share expert knowledge,** and it would be nice if they include a mention of your business or latest project when they run the story. Even if they don't, frequent appearances in the news media make you an authority, and people will have more trust in doing business with you.

## 3. Learn the Names of Those Who Are Most Likely to Use Your Releases, and Add Their Contact Info to You List.

Now that we've found an outlet, find the person most likely to be interested in your release. Features editor? Sports editor? Metro news? Enter their names, phone numbers, and contact info into your growing directory.  Access the last several issues of each publication either online or through your public library. If you've never used a public library (also known as a pre-Windows database), they have a wealth of current information, and trained staff that are often eager to help you learn to use their system to find answers.

Skim each issue, looking for clues on how that publication uses comment from local experts. For the individual staffers you've selected look for a trend in their work. What are they getting right? What do they seem to be missing?  Many publications now list the email address for each reporter at the end of the story. Capture it, and send the reporter a compliment about a recent story. The one that really strokes any journalist's ego is "You really showed me a side of that issue I hadn't considered before." This appeals to a journalists sense of fairness, balance and their sense of duty to educate the public about complex issues.

When I worked with **WBAI-FM** in New York, a left-progressive station, one of the reporters did a series on pending legislation to raise the minimum wage and the various ramifications this would have for the city's poorest workers. By the end of the series, we realized it would be a tough choice between the working poor making a little more money but having fewer jobs available or more jobs at a lower wage. The decision no longer seemed the slam-dunk it did at the outset, not even in a news department left-heavy with avowed Marxists. All that was clear is that either way, the poor were going to get screwed. It was a showpiece of fairness, accuracy, and balance.

## 4. Develop A Dossier For Each

Whether the master spy of your generation is James Bond, Jason Bourne, Annie Walker or Michael Westin, here's where you begin the process of developing a dossier on a stranger.

The attached dossier asks for about 60 pieces of information. If you can know the person, understand what makes him or her tick, you will have a better idea.

Some of the information you'll be able to find fairly easily. Other points will require long friendship. But that's our point - to genuinely get to know the media to whom you will submit releases, and get on the same wavelength so you are eventually regarded as a reliable, accessible expert in your chosen field.

The way NOT to do it is to send them the Dossier Template and ask them to fill it out when they have a moment! You don't even want them to know you're gathering information on them, so be covert! You'll soon realize that this is a good way to record information on friends, so you don't forget birthdays or anniversaries again.

As you get to actually know these people, they will open up to you. Chances are, you will never fill in **all** the blanks on more than five people. But in trying to, you can show genuine interest in their lives and experiences. This is the equivalent of doing a deal on the golf course or tennis court - most journalists don't have the time or resources for either pursuit!

Why would you bother spending that much time developing a relationship of trust with a reporter at a small town weekly? Because if they stay there, they'll be a big fish in a small pond. And if they go to a major market as their career develops, you'll have a friend in a major market that already thinks well of you. It's a win-win deal.

## 5. Offer To Help Them With Their Biggest Problems.

After you've established some background on your prospective contact, make contact. Ask question that show you have some genuine interest in journalism. look, the biggest problem facing the profession as I write this is the continuing demise of old-style print journalism. Fewer and fewer households subscribe to physical newspapers and magazines anymore. As a result, many outlets are downsizing their staffs, and nobody is certain where the ax will fall next. Every journalist has an increasing need to be seen by his or her superior as productive, resourceful, with a list of reliable sources.

Back in 2005 I was asked to organize a Media Day event for the community leadership course offered by my local chamber of commerce. In previous years, the local weekly newspaper editor and radio station manager had been invited. I invited them, of course, but also invited the regional daily paper and TV station to send a speaker. The news director of the TV station came 125 miles to speak to perhaps two dozen people, who wondered what magic or arm-twisting had been involved. What they didn't realize is that the TV news director, the expert from afar, was EAGER for these invitations to build contacts for both advertising and news sources in this part of their viewing region. In 1997, my news director would tell me to go to the next county and bring back at least a dozen usable stories: hard news, crime, politics, features, whatever. Long gone are those days when a news outlet had a surplus of people to send out on a random search for any newsworthy story. Today, each reporter tries to do the work of three, and make it look easy. YOUR job is to hand it to them, gift-wrapped and ready to run!

Why go to all this trouble? Remember that publicity has a long shelf life; it can lodge in peoples' memories waiting to be reactivated and revived long after a specific media exposure.

When I ran a large martial arts studio in northern New Jersey, we spent our limited advertising budget on a barrage of 30-second cable TV ads, a very economical option. Viewers don't classify and retain advertising messages based on how expensive the medium might have been; all TV commercials play out on the same screen. They ran for about a month. Years later, as we asked walk-ins how they heard about us, they usually said it was by the TV ads. When we asked when they saw it, the response was always "a few days/weeks ago." That's because when they saw a trigger for martial arts, their minds replayed the commercials, which they had probably seen dozens of times. They hadn't seen it on cable in the last week, they had seen it again in their minds!

# The Golden Rolodex: Developing Your Media Contacts

**Your most valuable asset in any business is the set of relationships you build with influential decision makers who will take your call; we call this collection the "Golden Rolodex."**

In any corporation, losing a sales director or other key manager means the risk of losing the Golden Rolodex of relationships that person has built up over time in that market. The same is true in journalism: you are only as good as your sources. A reporter who's new to an area needs to build connections fast. That means new reporters need you and your information almost as much as you need them.

Start by identifying reporters who have covered stories in your field of expertise. Begin filling in the information listed in the attached **Dossier Template.**

For media outlets, find out what they publish: their requirements, policies, and preferred contact methods. Don't trust your memory, write it down! See how extensively these outlets use **experts** in their pieces, and the type and length of direct quotes they include.

Dedicate a specific amount of time each week to work on researching the media in your target community and building your Golden Rolodex. Use that time to identify outlets, people, and subjects, and later to prepare materials to send to the media. Also use it to contact people in the media and to update your media lists. And remember that media jobs are very insecure with a high turnover. Update your list every three months or so to keep it current.

Do you have to know somebody in the media before you start? No! It helps, but you don't need to "know somebody" to get started. You don't have to know talk show hosts, producers, editors, to get started. But if you want to be more than a one-shot wonder, start cultivating relationships with these contacts as you make them. I have been on dozens of radio and TV talk shows and my releases have appeared in many newspapers where I didn't know a soul before the first appearance. I built the relationships after the initial publicity. You also don't need a publicity agency, a PR agency or a booking agency. What you need is a genuinely newsworthy hook.

## Letters To The Editor

Letter writing, along with penmanship, is becoming a lost art, like scrimshaw. Look at your local and regional "Letters" sections. Many newspapers have trouble filling that section with people who don't sound like wing-nut ideologues. This is a great way to let the outlets know who you are and check out your writing. However, it's important that you don't try to turn it into a news release. Choose a topic the pertains to your area of expertise. Perhaps you're in the insurance field and an insurance related bill is coming before the state assembly. You can present the likely results of passage or rejection. Better yet, present both probable results, as even-handedly as possible, without taking a side. This will gain you attention (editors and reporters at other outlets will see it, too) as an authority on that subject.

# Becoming Genuinely Newsworthy

**"Will our audience care about this story? Why?" If the answer is no, or I don't know, you're done. What you are offering to the media is your expertise wrapped in a genuine, newsworthy story. You need to familiarize yourself with what makes a story newsworthy, and then offer it in a way that makes you stand out from the pack. Think first like the audience, secondly like the editor, and thirdly like the source of information the outlet will want to return to again and again.**

Journalists are pulled in many directions each day. Time is valuable. You'll have a tough time getting any interest in your attention for your story idea.

**Don't explain events, anticipate trends**. Another way to think of this is that you are the course of a series of stories instead of a one-shot deal. Think of the letters to the editor example above. Connect your story to a current social, business, or political trend. Let's say your company has or will help a local business upgrade to something edgy like cloud-based web site and services. Base your release not on the local aspect, but on the trend itself and its larger implication.

Explain the trend, find information that supports the need for this innovation, the advantages and disadvantages, and what it means in the long run for the people and institutions in your community.

**Localize a regional, national or global story, and regionalize or nationalize a local angle.** Show your community and its media what their place a role might be after the new trend takes hold.

**Be The Different Voice**. When a big stories break, there's usually a lock-step of pundits chorusing of similar opinions on the implications. The media is always looking for a way to balance a story. If you are the odd man out, the minority opinion, you may get a place at the table just by offerings a different view.

Have facts at hand to back up what you say, but hold that hand in reserve. Expect to have your figures questioned (by any good journalist), so don't lead with numbers. Credible statistics and surveys underscore your story, but you need the story first.

**Watch The Calendar!**  We used to joke that Christmas stresses so many people because it comes at a different time each year. Think a few months ahead, and plant your story ideas in the minds of your target media early. Many outlets "sandbag" or "store up" undated stories for use during anticipated "slow news" periods.

**Get To The Point!** Your media contacts are always up against deadline pressure, and time is a valuable commodity. One of my cousins from Nashville called a New York City news room to offer a story on a Native American burial ground dispute. He began with the pleasantries that would be normal when cold-calling a business prospect in the South, and they almost hung up on him for wasting their time! Even though there may be a little regional variation, don't dawdle or engage in small talk. Give them information quickly, and when you promise more, deliver it on time as promised.

**Do Their Work, Let Them Sign It.** Because of their killer workload, news media people always need help finding stories, new angles, putting stories together, researching, documenting and substantiating them, and then meeting deadlines. In other words, they need help with every step of the process. Part of being their new best buddy is to pretty much do their whole job for them, then let them take full credit.

When I did publicity for my first book in 1985, I sent dozens of news releases which amounted to completed stories, ready for publication. One reporter - another "old school" type - actually came to interview me, and wanted me to substantiate quotes from various public officials and astronauts. I mentioned that I was surprised and impressed at his diligence; he replied that any journalist worth the title would do the same. I agreed - and he was floored when I revealed that *all* of his competitors had run the release verbatim as a story! (This happens more than you might think. Look for any print story that has "staff" or "staff report" instead of a by-line.)

**Be The Fan Club:** When you read an article, or see or hear a feature on your area of expertise (whether or not it's good or you agree with the spin of the story), send the reporter and/or producer a note or an e-mail stating how much you enjoyed the piece. You're not lying, you DID enjoy the piece, because it identified for you which reporter handles your specialty area. Everyone loves to have their efforts appreciated, but very few readers or viewers ever do that, and so your name will be remembered. This is part of "Stroking the Media." In fact, many media people will ask you directly if you are familiar with their work. If you say yes, mention a particular story. If the answer is no, you're just another huckster looking for free publicity.

There are any number of ways you can write a releases about your business that will get you into the **business section** (a good start, but you eventually want to break out into the front news and opinion section):

- Launching new product or service (as I have done with this product!)
- Joint venture with another business.
- Updates on a product of yours, or award of a patent.
- Changes to your business, including policies or personnel.
- Star Quality: news release referring to a famous client.
- Announce an upcoming media appearance.
- Conquering or beating your business competition. Be diplomatic and tasteful.
- Holds/Conducts/Hosts a contest or sweepstakes.
- Buys/Orders new business equipment, especially if your will be the first in the region.
- Builds/Constructs a new business building.

- Starting, removing or discontinuing a part of business.
- Acquires/Obtains a business or products rights.
- How you overcame a business obstacle - especially if it's one plaguing other businesses.
- Decreases/Lowers a price.
- Revealing or exposing a business trade secret. "Soylent Green is made from people!"
- Introducing a new product/service/business.
- You might construct a media article about broadcasting a class or teleseminar.
- Releases about how you are helping out the local community.
- A hires/appoints a new employee. Medical offices do this all the time.
- Outsourcing may be a bad word in some places, but your could have a release about outsourcing a type of job within the target community.
- You can honor or memorialize a deceased employee or customer, especially one well known in the community.
- Celebrating a business milestone, or the anniversary of a major event in recent, like a disaster that struck the community, recalling what your company did to help.
- How you are avoiding a negative situation/problem recently in the news... tainted foods, for example.
- Teaching a local business or special skills class/workshop.
- New strategies to lessen your business's environmental impact.
- Relocation or expansion into a new community.
- Predict a future trend, back it up with projected local impact.
- You may produce news information about donating to a charity, or sponsoring a charity event.
- Discover a new technology, or a new use for an existing product.
- Your business has won a prestigious award or competition.
- Hold a "retirement party" for a product that you've decided to discontinue. Conversely, hold an "out of retirement party" for a discontinued product you've decided to re-introduce.
- Media cannibalism: you can issue release for a local outlet about being featured in a national or international media outlet.

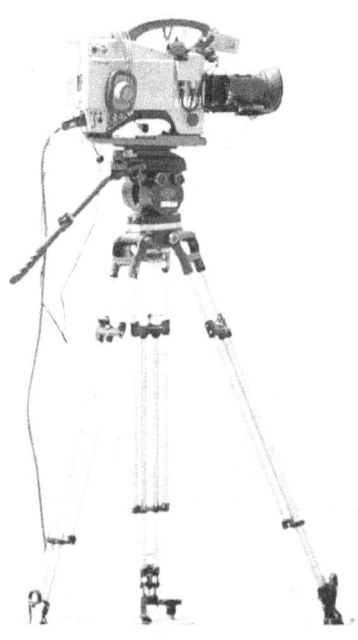

# Writing The "Anchorman" News Release

You've probably notice by now that I use the term "news release" where most use "press release". Back when I was a news anchor, there was a great rivalry between print and broadcast outlets. "Press" literally referred to printing presses, and in the opinion of broadcast journalists, was and obsolete term. We spoke of ourselves as news media and received news releases. Use whichever you prefer.

Here's one instance where the difference becomes crucial. It frequently happens in live media that someone hands the anchor a bulletin or story to "read cold": simply open mouth and read. Unfortunately, writers more accustomed to writing for the eye (print reader) rather than for the ear (broadcast listener) may unintentionally use a tongue-twister or two. I remember my first broadcast in 1971, when a wire service story from Belfast reported "a British soldier was shot in the shoulder." Also, because the audience doesn't have the luxury of re-reading an awkward or confusing phrase until it makes sense, broadcast writing **must** be understood on first hearing. You're not writing a novel, or trying to impress anyone with your literary skills. You goal should be to write a news story that could be handed to an anchor and read cold, and be instantly clear both to the anchor and the audience.

I'll give an example from another one of my professional heroes. Unlike Murrow or Cronkite, you may not recognize the name **Don Hewitt,** best known as the creator of **60 Minutes.** Strangely for someone not a radio veteran, he grasped the power of the spoken word to carry the story, and insisted that **60 Minutes** pieces be written well enough that they would make perfect sense if the picture went out. To that he added what became the trademark of the show - a close-up of the news source so tight that the top of the head and often the bottom of the chin was cut off. The expressions of the eyes and mouth, today known as **micro-gestures,** would be a factor in letting the audience decide if the speaker was being honest and open, or concealing something. In an era when so many newsmakers tried to finesse their way around a tough interview, the combination of tough questions and a tight close-up that would be seen by tens of millions has brought many memorable revelations since the show debuted in 1968.

Beginners often think you need some great writing skill to write a press release, that you have to have a degree in journalism or a background in literature. Nah! You just have to follow the main rule, **Get To The Point!**

> **Quick definition:** Both news verbiage and advertising verbiage are called **copy**. If you write advertising copy, you are a **copywriter.** If you write news copy, you are a **journalist.** When someone talks about copywriting, they mean writing to sell rather than inform. Copyrighting, however, means to place your writing under copyright protection. Confusing at first since they're pronounced the same way. "The **copywriter** spent the day **copyrighting** his copy."

Some of the worst press releases I've seen were written by great copywriters. The reason they are so bad is because copywriters are writing advertising copy. You don't need any special writing ability or any special skills, any background in journalism, media, or literature.

Let's get on to the release.

1. Build your release around a **compelling newsworthy hook**, and open with that hook.

2. The **SUBJECT** line of the email should begin with the words NEWS RELEASE in caps, followed by a title that makes it clear exactly what the release is about.

3. Includes a brief summary statement listing each item sent. ("News Release plus 2 photos")

4. Make it clear if the release is for IMMEDIATE RELEASE or is EMBARGOED until a specified time and date. The second makes it an **Advance Release**, and all legitimate news outlets will honor that condition.

5. Post your release in the BODY of the email. This is because many news outlets won't open an attachment from an unknown sender for fear of viruses and malware.

6. At the top right of the release, add your contact information: real name, and phone number where a live person will answer, not an answering machine or voicemail. If you carry a cell phone most of the time, give that number. Until you establish yourself with the media, they probably won't try to call more than twice.

7. Write your release as a readable, **voiceable** story, ready to be spoken on air or printed. For this to work, your release must be coherent and clear enough to make sense on first reading or hearing. That's why I call it an "anchorman" release.

8. The **inverted pyramid** style of writing is standard. The most important facts belong at the top, less important comments at the bottom. When editors needs to rim a piece to fit available space, they simply trim from the bottom. If you wait until the end to make a dramatic point, as you learned in creative writing class, it may be lost.

9. The extreme form of this is "head and body" style. The first sentence gives all of the important facts of the story, and can stand alone as a headline. The next two lines, the "shoulder", contain supporting information. The head and shoulders tells the whole story. The body simply gives depth. The advantage to broadcasters is that these stories could be stacked up, and the first line alone read when it was time for a quick headline update. The advantage in a news release is that the recipient knows immediately if your release is of interest.

10. Give the diagnosis, not the entire lab report. Speak in brief slogans and catchy phrases. Write and talk in **sound bites**. These are quotes that capsulize what you want the audience to remember. Aim for 5 second, 10 second, and 20 second bites.

11. Do NOT end the release with the old printer's code, - 30 - , unless you want the oldest person on staff to laugh thinking you've read too many Dashiel Hammett novels. The younger newsies will be looking for the missing 29 pages of the release.

12. Don't write a thinly veiled advertisement for your products or services; those are tossed almost immediately. Tell a story instead... a NEWS story!

13. DO NOT send supporting materials such as media kits, surveys, and statistics, but indicate that they are available upon request.

14. If you have a web site or blog, post the complete text and photos there. Photos should be at least 150dpi resolution, 300dpi is better. Include the URL of the page with your release; some outlets prefer to go to a web page and copy the text and download the photos rather than accept attachments in email.

Here's an example, an article that ran in several West Kentucky news outlets in 2008. I've included a transcript of the text.

# 'Stone Diplomacy' links two tribal communities in Kentucky, Morocco

**BRIAN WILKES**

The Cherokee community of western Kentucky has established a unique relationship with the Berber community in Morocco. The contact and a traditional exchange of gifts were initiated by Brian Wilkes, a Cherokee language instructor in Marion.

"In February," Wilkes said, "a college friend, Bonnie Rankin, told me she would be traveling to Morocco and visiting the Berber tribal areas, escorted by Smithsonian Institute staff and a renowned historian."

The Berbers are a tribal people whose lands once stretched from Mauritania on the Atlantic to Libya on the Mediterranean, and are related to the Phoenicians and Carthaginians.

"I recalled old Cherokee migration legends that suggest an ancient connection with North Africa, and the DNA markers in most Cherokee mixed-bloods that support the story. My own DNA test shows Berber matches," Wilkes said.

"In my dealings with tribal elders around the Americas over the past 20 years, one common custom is the exchange of stones. Each elder ends up with a bundle of ordinary looking rocks, which maintain that elder's connection with the people who gave the stone, and their lands."

The idea came to Wilkes that this was an opportunity to exchange stones with what might have been the ancient Cherokee homeland. He went to Mantle Falls in Livingston County, an important site along the Trail of Tears, and found a small stone. He then wrote a letter in English and French explaining the situation and tradition, bundled the stone in a beautiful deerskin pouch, and sent the stone and a letter in English and French to Rankin, who carried the bundle on her Moroccan adventure.

"My people, the Cherokee," he wrote, "believe that we were saved from a volcano and flood by sailing west on reed boats, following a seven-pointed star, and we believe we must always live in the mountains near cedar trees in case the world floods again; and we called the mountains Attala. We tell stories that our ancient homeland still exists beyond the sea."

The seven-pointed star is important in North African tradition, and is sometimes called the "Star of the West." The mountains in Morocco are called Atlas, and were famous for their cedar trees. Natives of the Azores, Canaries, and other Atlantic islands told similar flood evacuation stories. Traditional Cherokees believe that we should try to live in mountains with cedars, both to remind us of the old country and to give us an advantage in the next flood.

Rankin, through an interpreter, explained the letter to Amina, the mistress of a Berber home in the rural Ourika Valley southeast of Marrakech, who hosted part of the trek. She immediately recognized the custom, brought a stone from her courtyard garden, and presented her stone in exchange, adding hugs and the French style kiss on both cheeks for Rankin. Amina then carefully placed the Kentucky stone in the same garden spot her gift had just vacated.

The Kentucky stone now sits in a Berber garden in Morocco, and the Berber stone, which arrived in March, now sits in a Cherokee garden in Marion. Wilkes says that the stone is a constant reminder of the ancient oral histories and the migration sagas of the Cherokee people, as well as the lesson that connections between people require someone to reach out first.

"We can only wonder what the Berber family thinks when they gaze at the Kentucky stone," he said. "What story will they share with generations to come?"

As you review this, ask yourself what product or service I'm promoting. Can't find it? Then it must be a legitimate, non-commercial NEWS story that belongs in the news section, not the advertisements... which is exactly where it ran in each outlet that used it!

Give up? I'm NOT promoting a business, product or service. I'm establishing myself as a source on Native American / Cherokee cultural matters, and a language instructor. I make no reference to my online language course or publications. Several interested parties contacted me through the newspapers or looked me up (I lived in a very small town). It even led to a recommendation for a seat on the state's Native American Heritage Commission.

May 3, 2008 - The Times Leader, Princeton, KY

# "Stone Diplomacy" Links Two Tribal Communities In Kentucky, Morocco.

The Cherokee community of Western Kentucky has established a unique relationship with the Berber community in Morocco. The contact and traditional exchange of gifts were initiated by Brian Wilkes, the Cherokee language instructor in Marion.

"In February," Wilkes said, "a college friend, bonnie Rankin, told me she would be traveling to Morocco and visiting the Berber tribal areas, escorted by Smithsonian Institute staff and a renowned historian."

The Berbers are a tribal people whose lands wants stretched from Mauritania on the Atlantic to Libya on the Mediterranean, and are related to the ancient Phoenicians and Carthaginians.

"I recalled old Cherokee migration legends that suggest an ancient connection with North Africa, and the DNA markers in most Cherokee mixed bloods support that story. My own DNA test shows the Berber matches," Wilkes said.

"In my dealings with tribal Elders around the Americas over the past 20 years, one common custom is the exchange of stones. Each builder ends up with a bundle of ordinary looking rocks, which maintain that Elders connection with the people who gave the stone, and their lands."

The idea came to Wilkes that this was an opportunity to exchange stones with what might have been the ancient Cherokee homeland. He went to Mandy falls in Livingston county, an important site on the Trail of Tears, and found a small stone. He then wrote a letter in English and French explaining the situation and tradition, bundled the stone in a ceremonial deerskin pouch, and sent the stone and letter in English and French to Rankin, who carried the bundle on her Moroccan journey.

"My people, the Cherokee," he wrote, "believe that we were saved from a volcano and flood by sailing west on reed boats, following a seven-pointed star, and we believe we must always live in the mountains near cedar trees in case the world floods again. We call the mountains 'attala'. We tell stories that our ancient homeland still exists beyond the sea."

The seven-pointed star is important in north African tradition, and is sometimes called "the star of the west." The mountains in Morocco are called Atlas, and were famous for their cedar trees. Natives of the Azores, canaries, and other Atlantic islands told similar flood evacuation stories. Traditional Cherokees believe that we should try to live in mountains with cedars, both to remind us of the old country and to give us an advantage in the next flood.

Rankin, through an interpreter, explained of the letter to Amina, the mistress of the Berber home in the rural Ourika Valley southeast of Marrakech, who hosted part of the trek. She immediately recognize the custom, brought a stone from her courtyard garden, and presented her stone in exchange adding hugs and the French style kiss on both cheeks for Rankin. Amina then carefully placed the Kentucky stone in the same garden spot her gift had just vacated.

The Kentucky stone now sits in a Berber garden in Morocco, and the Berber stone, which arrived in march, now sits in the Cherokee garden in Marion. Wilkes says that the stone is a constant reminder of the ancient oral histories and migration saga as of the Cherokee people, as well as the lesson that connections between peoples require that someone reach out first.

"We can only wonder what the Berber family thinks when they gaze at the Kentucky stone," he said. "What story will they share with generations to come?"

- SAMPLE NEWS RELEASE -

(Email subject line)
**NEWS RELEASE : Marion Tourism Web Site Top-Ranked in Major Search Engines.**

(Email body)
*name of intended recipient:*

*Here is a release plus links to 2 photos. Let me know if you need more information. I'm an authority in this subject, and can make you look good!*

*Best regards,*
*Brian Wilkes*

**FOR FURTHER INFORMATION CONTACT:**
Brian Wilkes, Web Developer, brian@xxx.com, xxx-xxx-xxxx
__ ___, Tourism Director, director@xxx.gov, xxx-xxx-xxxx

**For IMMEDIATE release:**

## Marion Tourism Web Site Gets Top Rankings In Major Search Engines

.....

**MARION, KY:** A six-month effort to boost search engine rankings for the Marion Tourism Commission's web site has paid off with top rankings in all the major search engines.

Web developer Brian Wilkes reported at Thursday's Tourism Commission meeting that the web site www.MarionKentucky.gov now ranks in the top spots on Altavista, MSN, and Yahoo search engines for the search term "Marion Kentucky". Before the search engine optimization, the city's own tourism site could barely be found.

"Town and location names are among of the most competitive terms for search engine placement," said Wilkes. "Large directory companies buy up domain names and pump money into making sure search engines will see their sites. These are often directories for realtors, auto lots or advertising services, and often have no real connection with the town they claim to represent."

The site gets visits from around the world, thanks in part to a built in translator that lets the viewer see the site in any of 11 languages. The tourism map of the Amish region is downloaded over 60 times each week.

Wilkes added, "Now we need to focus on raising our ranking for other phrases... hunting, antiques, and quilts for example,"

[end release]

# Following Up, Professionally

Unless the specific news outlet tells you differently, submit the release by email.

Follow up by email in 24 hours to confirm that they received your release. If they have not replied in three days, follow up by phone (they may not be receiving your e-mails) to inquire if they have set an air date or publication date for the piece, and to ask if they need anything more. This confirms that you're a real person interested in *their* outlet, not just a submission service sending the same piece to thousands of outlets.

If they are still non-committal, they aren't sparing your feelings, they're either overwhelmed with the volume of news or there's a problem with your piece. Follow up a third time, by phone, and see if you can smoke out the objection. However, on the fourth follow up, you're officially a **pest.**

Keep all of the follow-ups brief and to the point. Don't take it personally. And don't try to convince them they made the wrong decision; that moves you from the category of semi-journalist and one of the True Brotherhood back into the category of huckster. Thank them for taking their valuable time to review it, and move on.

Treat **every mention** of your name or business as a priceless favor, and every rejection as "nothing personal". That will be how they regard it, and by accepting the same attitude you'll show you're a professional who understands them and their business needs.

**The next news deadline is never far off. They still *need* you!**

# SUMMARY: The Rules

- Thou shalt not BORE! After each sentence, ask yourself "Who cares?"

- News departments and advertising departments are separate.

- Journalists believe they are public servants, not entertainers. Help them serve.

- Become a colleague helping them serve the public, not a huckster using them for media access.

- Journalism is a highly competitive field. There is no job security. Help them develop new sources of reliable information… starting with you.

- Write a NEWS release, not a commercial.

- Don't say anything you can't back up if questioned.

- Don't make editors guess what your story idea is about.

- Press releases are **one** page. That means 300 - 500 words. No exceptions!

- Put contact information for a live, responsive human in the upper right.

- Use "head and shoulders style" - Headline, plus two sentences that tell the whole story. The rest is just details. Better yet, tell the whole story in your headline.

- Use inverted pyramid style.

- Black text on white is professional. A discrete letterhead or logo isn't awful, but no e-mail that looks like patterned stationery.

- The purpose of the press release is to convince the editor that you have a legitimate news story, and get them to PHONE YOU, or at worst, to e-mail you.

# Four Factors To NEVER Forget!
## by ROBERT YEHLING

I remember the greatest single day of my career as a publicist like it was yesterday. On Day Three of the 1986 Billabong Pro, a world tour surfing event, the waves came up at Oahu's Waimea Bay. Way up. Eventually, the faces exceeded 40 feet. The world's best surfers paddled out and tackled the surf with varying degrees of success. Several had great rides. One almost drowned from being held down by a wave. Another got blown off the wave by the downdraft of a helicopter hovering overhead.

I was partially responsible for the latter incident. Earlier, while watching the monstrous waves, an idea occurred to me. I approached Bob Hurley, then the president of Billabong USA, and said, "You know, if we can get a photographer and a video guy into a helicopter, I might be able to get the footage around the world overnight – and to the national news and morning shows. Would you spring for it if I get it set up?"

Now the Founder, President and CEO of Hurley International, Bob Hurley isn't one of the legends (and one of the truly nice men) of the beachwear and activewear industry for nothing. Two hours later, our helicopter was knocking one surfer off his board – and our cameramen were shooting the video and photos that, we hoped, would provide the only kind of promotion Hurley really cared about: men riding giant waves at the contest his company funded. You do that, he reasoned, and people will buy the clothes and the image.

On that day, Billabong began its climb to becoming a $1 billion-a-year company.

After our hired guns landed and returned with the footage, we rushed to KHON-TV in Honolulu. I sat on my hot new technological toy, a laptop computer, and banged out a press release. Then I wrote out the copy for a newer concept, a video news release. And finally, the coordinates for a satellite feed. Meanwhile, the photographer, who rode to Honolulu with me, practically received star status when I dropped him off at the *Honolulu Advertiser* offices. In exchange for giving them a couple photos to run, he received carte blanche to process his film there.

We FAXed the press release to my long contact list, and then sent up 30-second news clips and longer video pieces through KHON's satellite uplink. Remember, these were the days when the only people who held e-mail accounts worked for the Department of Defense.

The next day, like a spring bloom in the Sonoran desert, the Billabong Pro's big waves and the men who ride them appeared seemingly everywhere: the *Today Show, Good Morning America, CNN, ESPN, NBC News, World News Tonight,* and numerous network affiliates. The press release and photos ran on AP, UPI, Reuters, *USA Today,* and a couple dozen metro newspapers.

We hit a home run. Make that a grand slam. This moment defined my career as an event and athlete publicist, basically cornering the market of a quickly growing action sports industry for the next five years. Everyone who participated in the decision to hire the helicopter enjoyed significant bumps in their careers. Mainstream media coverage of surfing competition exploded. Which led to the reason why these companies sponsored events – to put their clothes on customers' bodies. While Ocean-Pacific and Quiksilver already had solid footholds in the marketplace in 1986, the Billabong Pro's "waves-seen-round-the-world" coverage busted open the doors for all the beachwear companies to receive mainstream lifestyle and fashion press. By the end of the decade, kids from Nebraska to Pittsburgh to Albuquerque were decked out in style … long before hip-hop gained a foothold.

So much has changed in the way we deliver news since that late November day in 1986. Now, we write press releases, email blast them to our destinations, often including video clips or photos, in one concise delivery from our laptops, desktops. Or tablets. Photos aren't developed in chemical soups; they're downloaded from digital cameras and then rendered or (gulp) Photoshopped before being sent on. The releases are even "smart releases", with links to further resources and contacts (which we'll address in a moment). And FAX machines? When is the last time you used one of those Cretacean machines? In 1986, they were saviors for those of us promoting events from different time zones.

In short, the old boots-on-the-ground strategy all veteran publicists remember from their longest, red-eyed days and nights seems to be passé. Why spend the day pitching media on the phone when you can reach them, and five thousand others, with an email blast? Why go over trends and developments with you when they've already read it in one of the two hundred media drop-offs the CEO Express portal offers? Why pinpoint one or two perfect photos to send when you can point them to a Flickr or Picasa site, or link them to the photographer's page? Why "work a contact" or "work a source," to use the parlance of the day, when you and I can go back and forth on email, texting, Facebook or LinkedIn and get the job done without even knowing what each other's voice sounds like – let alone what our faces look like?

Likewise, it would be so easy, and pleasing to the ego, to say that we scored our surf industry media breakthrough with boots-on-the-ground brilliance and genius. It would be even easier to say that the resulting coverage occurred because people saw our brilliance and wanted to be sure to pay it forward to their readers and audiences.

Nothing could be further from the truth. What *really* happened was a dynamic that holds just as true now as it did in 1986, and as it will when the publicists and promoters of 2030 deliver their news telepathically, or however it happens: **we took advantage of timing, newsworthiness, opportunity, and perception**. Those are A, B, C and D of catching and riding the publicity wave.

In our case, we held the event on a big-wave day – perfect **timing**. Because the waves were big enough to warrant Coast Guard and emergency management alerts on the coast, the event became **newsworthy**. We hired the helicopter to get the shots – **opportunistic**. And what do Americans dream of when they're beginning to enter the deep freeze of another winter? The hot sands and warm waters of Hawaii or another tropical clime. Our pictures gave it to them in a most thrilling way – **perception**. For thirty seconds on *The Today Show,* millions of viewers pictured themselves not chiseling ice off their windshields, but rubbing white sand off their sunburned bodies.

Public relations today utilizes the same principles. We completely believe in our event, cause, program, announcement, book, show or film, and we craft a message that motivates the media to publish or air the information. That same message, we hope, sufficiently informs our target audience to buy tickets, donate, purchase our products, sway or strengthen their opinion. If our information causes them to act, to make a choice of some kind, then we have been effective.

The keys to make this happen are the same four as always: **Timing. Opportunity. Newsworthiness. Perception.**

However, as mentioned, the tools are different. Very different. Today, when you launch a worthwhile PR campaign, you utilize a combination of most (if not all) of these resources:

- Email and phone contact lists

- Client databases

- Constant Contact or similar newsletter service

- Social media

- Email blasts

- Electronic press releases

- Video clips, transmitted as MPEGs

- Audio clips, transmitted as MP3 files or similar

- High-resolution (magazine print quality) photos, transmitted as JPGs

- Blogs and electronic blogs

Instead of operating from a image-conscious corporate office, with a staff that includes envelope stuffers and point people manning phones all day, you can do all of this from the comfort of your home office. Heck, when it comes right down to it, you can operate a highly efficient publicity campaign with a tablet and smartphone. Unlike your predecessors, who built their contacts brick by painstaking brick, you potentially do have the entire world at your beckoned call, through the Internet, ubiquitous social media sites like Facebook, and the incredible dynamic that happens when a message or product goes viral.

Out of all of these new resources and tools, there are three that still adhere to last-generation principles in order to ensure optimal success: two are email and phone contact lists. Keeping these continuously updated is essential to gaining the promotion and publicity you desire. Knowing the specific contact point for your release is just as vital; sending a book release to a news director will not get the job done. Furthermore, there are no excuses for keeping them updated – the information is instantaneous.

The other element, to which the rest of this chapter is devoted, is the press release. It is the foundation of all good publicity campaigns, yet among the most misunderstood documents to those trying to promote their businesses, books, services, events, causes or products. Some think – and God bless their confidence! – that their offering is a savior of the world, or at least their target customer. They write a release that proclaims that truth … and then wonder why no one bothers to run it. Others write shoddy, poorly constructed releases that fail to convey the message, and leave out important details. They, too, end up in the junk or trash bin. Still others write a brilliant release that breaks down their product or service in captivating detail – but forget to state its relevance in the big picture. Not good enough.

As you consider these shortcomings, let's jump quickly to the receiving end, the other side of the desk – the newspaper, magazine, website, television, radio or Internet radio journalist who is reviewing your release. Let's jump into their shoes. Gone, too, are their boots-on-the-ground days, their gumshoe days where they worked leads and stories like dogs to scoop their competitors and deliver the news. When I started out as a journalist in 1976, we had to type and retype – on a typewriter! – and write down quotes, make many calls, and call more people to check the accuracy on our stories. Remember Rolodexes? We didn't have Google.

Today, every time a journalist logs in at work, he or she has at their disposal the entire Internet, news blurbs coming in from Reuters and Associated Press, bookmarks to hundreds of sources in their field, and the ability to obtain information instantly through their social media or traditional contacts. In other words, they can fill their publications many times over without making any extra effort.

Your press release will require them to make the extra effort to give it space, and perhaps build a story around it. How are you going to convince them to lift a finger? How will you show them why your subject is of value or interest to their reader? Never have those two questions been more important to answer clearly than now, when the information glut is bigger than ever and the competition for print, air or online space greater than ever.

Remember the four keys to effective delivery of messages in public relations? This is when you bring them in, big time. No matter how killer your product or service, how potentially transforming it is to the world, if you do not present a picture of timeliness, newsworthiness, opportunity and perception that it can make an impact in the audience's life or marketplace NOW, then it will not work.

What happens when you combine these age-old public relations principles with a delivery technology that is cutting edge and perfect for the vast array of today's media? Quick answer: a result that can go viral and change the perception of your product or service overnight, not by rushing to TV stations and uploading satellite footage, but by connecting through your release and hitting "SEND". Once.

A platform that we're using at a new book and product publicity service, **Beacon Publicity**, illustrates this well. We start by working with press releases that are timely and relevant. In other words, if you write a press release about your book, you must go well beyond the contents of your book to explain its timeliness and relevance today. What events is it connected to? What social issues? What timely messages do the characters or subjects convey? What modern-day developments come to mind? In other words, tie the press release content as directly as possible to the headlines.

Next, we convert the print releases into "smart" releases. We embed links, either to your website or sites that provide further resources or information. We link to your Facebook, Twitter and Linked In sites (tip: if you're publicizing something, anything, maintain active accounts in all three social media arenas). If you have a grouping of photos on a gallery like Picasa or Flickr, we link to those. We also link to any audio files on your site, or video connected to the release topic (a big reason to maintain a YouTube account; videos tend to go viral on YouTube, which increases delivery of your message). You can do all of this yourself; it's easy. It's also necessary to rise above the very thick layers of competition.

The platform we use combines the best of both worlds – delivery of press releases to well-targeted media, and use of social media to spread the word into businesses and consumers. Our core platform, PRWeb, transmits every release to up to 30,000 points. You name the type of media – and the location – and PRWeb downloads to computers there. Wire services, newspapers, magazines, book publishers, online media, television, search engines … all of it. By pre-sorting through media subjects, or categories, the point is sharpened even more so that the right target media receive the release.

What happens then? In the old days – when I started in publicity – the receiving reporter had to type in the release (rather, or their intern, cub reporter or assistant).  Now, they read the release on their screen, decide they want to use it, and download it. For example, a release on the memoir *A Taste of Eternity* that we uploaded for author Martha Halda found its way onto the website of *50* different television stations. You can only imagine how the publishers then considering the near-death experience memoir reacted; the competition to pick it up suddenly became fierce. *Timeliness.* Within a few hours of receipt, your release could literally be sitting on hundreds of websites, with aggregators like Google News, Yahoo! News, the Huffington Post and others ready to launch it worldwide.

But that's not all. A good publicity platform needs to not only include the perception of reality – media relations – but also today's electronic reality – the social media world. If your release gets picked up by, say, 1,000 media points, and your Facebook and Twitter pages are hotlinked into the releases they upload to their sites, guess what? Hundreds of thousands, or up to many millions, of people suddenly have their first access to your Facebook and Twitter accounts. To wit: I wrote a release about a newsworthy recent blog series, and uploaded it. Within two days, my daily reads increased by *400%,* and my core subscribers by *300%.* In two days. Likewise, my Facebook and Twitter accounts grew.

And, at least with the Beacon service, everything is *accountable.* Reports are issued within 48 to 72 hours of the press release being sent. Do you know how many long-time public relations executives are amazed by that? To the point where they shake their weary heads? In the 1980s, here is how you determined how much coverage you received: you subscribed to everything, and then you hired a clip service, like Bacon's, for anywhere from $200 to $1,000 per month to track down everything else. It took up to three months. Now, it takes 48 to 72 hours, and the reports are auto-generated.

When we drew up publicity campaigns back in the day, our only concern was newspaper-magazine-television. And sometimes film, depending upon the subject. Now, with platforms like the combination mega-media service/social media outreach that Beacon Publicity offers, you can address a new scope that is truly the sign of our times: hitting online media, traditional media and the general public, simultaneously, right where they sit. In front of their computers, tablets or smartphones.

In closing, as you position and brand your business, product or service, and prepare to write that relevant press release that will be the core of your active public relations campaign, a quick pop-quiz: What are the four guiding principles of good public relations? Heard that question before? There's a reason: to memorize the answers and use them with everything you do.

Again, the four:

• **Timeliness**

• **Newsworthiness**

• **Opportunity**

• **Perception**

Looking forward to reading, hearing or seeing all about it!

ROBERT YEHLING is a long-time journalist, author, editor, and co-founder of Beacon Publicity, a book- and product-publicity service. He also founded Horizon Communications, the top public relations firm in the California beachwear industry in the 1980s and early 1990s. He's won Independent Publishing Book Awards in the media category for two books on writing, ***Writes of Life*** and ***The Write Time***. His newest book, ***Just Add Water: Clay Marzo's Mastery of the Ocean Through the Prism of Asperger Syndrome,*** will be published by Hougton Mifflin in Spring 2014.

He can be reached at 917-826-7880 or RYehling@WordJourneys.com

# FORMS for Your "Golden Rolodex"

## NEWS MEDIA CONTACT LIST

| CITY | Name, URL, Mailing Address | Phone/Fax | Email | Facebook/Twitter /LinkedIn |
|------|----------------------------|-----------|-------|----------------------------|
| Metropolis, KS | **Clark Kent**, city desk<br>Daily Planet<br>100 News Plaza, Metropolis KS | 1-618-SaveMe | clark.kent@planet.com | Facebook.com/CK101<br>MildMannered@Twitter.com<br>LinkedIn.com/krypton |
| | | | | |
| | | | | |
| | | | | |
| | | | | |
| | | | | |
| | | | | |
| | | | | |
| | | | | |
| | | | | |
| | | | | |
| | | | | |
| | | | | |
| | | | | |
| | | | | |
| | | | | |

# NEWS CONTACT DOSSIER

| Last UPDATED: |
| --- |
| NAME:<br>NICKNAME: |
| OUTLET NAME:<br>OUTLET ADDRESS:<br><br>WEB SITE:<br>FACEBOOK:<br>TWITTER:<br><br>WORK PHONE:<br>CELL PHONE:<br>WORK EMAIL: |
| PERSONAL |
| HOME ADDRESS:<br>HOME PHONE:<br>PERSONAL EMAIL:<br>WEB SITE:<br>FACEBOOK:<br>TWITTER:<br>LINKED IN:<br>BIRTH DATE:<br>BIRTH PLACE:<br>HOMETOWN (if other than birthplace)<br>HEIGHT:        WEIGHT: |
| EDUCATION |
| HIGH SCHOOL[S]:<br>YEAR GRADUTATED:<br>PROUDEST HIGH SCHOOL ACHIEVEMENT: |
| COLLEGE[S]:<br>YEAR GRADUTATED:<br>DEGREE:<br>HONORS:<br>FRATERNITY/SORORITY:<br>SPORTS:<br>ACTIVITES:<br>PROUDEST COLLEGE ACHIEVEMENT:<br>IF DIDN'T ATTEND COLLEGE, IS HE/SHE SENSITIVE ABOUT IT?: |
| MILITARY SERVICE |
| BRANCH<br>HIGHEST RANK |

RESERVE STATUS
HONORS
ATTITUDE TOWARD MILITARY SERVICE?

## FAMILY

SPOUSE'S NAME
SPOUSE's OCCUPATION

SPOUSE'S EDUCATION

SPOUSE'S INTERESTS
ANNIVERSARY
CHILDREN, IF ANY, NAMES/AGES

CHILDREN'S EDUCATION

CHILDREN'S INTERESTS (HOBBIES, PROBLEMS, ETC.)

## BUSINESS BACKGROUND

PREVIOUS NEWS EXPERIENCE (Most recent first)

COMPANY
LOCATION
TITLE
DATES                    [copy this section as needed]

PREVIOUS POSITIONS AT PRESENT COMPANY:
TITLE
DATES

STATUS SYMBOLS IN OFFICE

PROFESSIONAL OR TRADE ASSOCIATIONS

OFFICES HELD OR HONORS

WHAT DO YOU FEEL IS HIS/HER LONG RANGE BUSINESS OBJECTIVE IN JOURNALISM?

WHAT DO YOU FEEL IS HIS/HER IMMEDIATE BUSINESS OBJECTIVE?

WHAT DO YOU THINK IS OF GREATEST CONCERN TO THE CUSTOMER AT THIS TIME-THE WELFARE OF THE COMPANY OR HIS/HER OWN PERSONAL WELFARE?

DOES THE CUSTOMER THINK OF THE PRESENT OR THE FUTURE?

SPECIAL INTERESTS

CLUB, **PROFESSIONAL** ASSOCIATIONS OR SERVICE CLUBS (Masons, Kiwanis, etc.)
_____

POLITICALLY ACTIVE?_____PARTY_____IMPORTANT TO CUSTOMER

ACTIVE IN COMMUNITY?_____HOW?

RELIGION_____ACTIVE

HIGHLY CONFIDENTIAL/SENSITIVE ITEMS <u>NOT</u> TO BE DISCUSSED WITH CUSTOMER (i.e.: Divorce, AA Member, etc.)
ON WHAT SUBJECTS (OUTSIDE OF BUSINESS) DOES THE CUSTOMER HAVE STRONG FEELINGS?

<u>LIFESTYLE</u>

MEDICAL HISTORY (Current Condition of Health)

DOES CUSTOMER DRINK?_____IF YES, WHAT AND HOW MUCH?

IF NO, IS CUSTOMER OFFENDED BY OTHERS DRINKING?

DOES CUSTOMER SMOKE?_____IF NO, OBJECT TO OTHERS?
_____
_____

FAVORITE PLACES FOR LUNCH_____ DINNER

FAVORITE ITEMS ON MENU

_____  _____
DOES CUSTOMER OBJECT TO HAVING ANYONE BUY HIS/HER MEAL?
HOBBIES AND RECREATIONAL INTERESTS

VACATION HABITS

SPECTATOR SPORTS INTEREST:  SPORTS AND TEAMS
_____

WHAT KIND OF CAR(S)

CONVERSATIONAL INTERESTS

WHOM DOES THE CUSTOMER SEEM ANXIOUS TO IMPRESS?
_____

HOW DOES HE/SHE WANT TO BE SEEN BY THOSE PEOPLE?

WHAT ADJECTIVES WOULD YOU USE TO DESCRIBE THE CUSTOMER?

_____

WHAT IS HE/SHE MOST PROUD OF HAVING ACHIEVED?

_____

WHAT DO YOU FEEL IS CUSTOMER'S LONG RANGE PERSONAL OBJECTIVE?
WHAT DO YOU FEEL IS THE CUSTOMER'S IMMEDIATE PERSONAL GOAL?

THE CUSTOMER AND YOU

WHAT MORAL OR ETHICAL CONSIDERATIONS ARE INVOLVED WHEN YOU WORK WITH THIS CUSTOMER?
DOES CUSTOMER FEEL ANY OBLIGATION TO YOU, YOUR COMPANY OR YOUR COMPETITION?
IF SO, WHAT?
DOES THE PROPOSAL YOU PLAN TO MAKE TO HIM/HER REQUIRE THE CUSTOMER TO CHANGE A HABIT OR TAKE AN ACTION THAT IS CONTRARY TO CUSTOM?
IS HE/SHE PRIMARILY CONCERNED ABOUT THE OPINION OF OTHERS?

IS HE/SHE VERY SELF-CENTERED?_____HIGHLY ETHICAL?

WHAT ARE THE KEY PROBLEMS AS THE CUSTOMER SEES THEM?
WHAT ARE THE PRIORITIES OF THE CUSTOMER'S MANAGEMENT?
CAN YOU HELP WITH THESE PROBLEMS?_____HOW?

Copy these pages as needed.

# Mark Ress interviews Brian Wilkes about

# "Stroking The Media"

**MARK RESS:** Hey everybody! This is Mark Ress with Brother Brian Wilkes, the creator of **Stroking The Media**. I've known Brother Brian Wilkes for many, many years. He's been a good friend, a spiritual adviser and nothing less than a professional when it comes to what he does. He's actually just been able to share some of that knowledge with me throughout the years. Because of that, I was able to get myself booked on a radio show here in Los Angeles, and now I'm in talks with the program director and radio station owner to have my own tech hour here in Los Angeles. So, the inventor of **Stroking The Media**, his brainchild, Brother Brian Wilkes. Thanks for being here today.

**BRIAN WILKES:** Thank you for having me, Mark.

**MR:** I'm going to jump right in because I know people are going to want to get right down to the nitty gritty of this bonus. They don't want to have all this fluff. Let's go ahead and jump right in to this because so many "IMers" have their own opinions of tools out there like blog talk radio, podcasting and that's not what we're talking about. I have a really big pet peeve when people really think that the Internet bubble is such a huge market, when it's really small compared to other market outside the Internet bubble. One being radio, right? Radio, traditional radio. Not stuff like **Blog Talk Radio**.

**BW:** Not only traditional radio, but perhaps more importantly, we forget that there's still a print medium out there. There are a lot of people who read magazines, who read newspapers. Not only that, but these newspapers, whether they are actually paper newspapers or online newspapers, have fantastic credibility, have fantastic authority and perhaps more importantly, they are read by other journalists.

I had a case where one newspaper, a little local newspaper did something about me, and with no further action on my part, the big regional paper picked it up, called me, set up an interview, set up a photographer simply because they read that original piece.

41

**MR:** Talking about leveraging that exposure right? You didn't do anything and they came to you.

**BW:** Absolutely! And that's my whole point. Get them to come to you! Get them to recognize you as a news source, as an authority in your field, and a good source of continuing news content for them.

**MR:** Not only that, but it gets them to recognize you as the authority in your niche. Like that one book that I believe was written by **Elsom Eldridge**, "The Instant Expert" or something like that.

**BW:** That's Elsom Eldridge, Jr. - **"The Obvious Expert"**. Absolutely! Great resource to have!

**MR**: This gives you, 100% correct, gives you credibility. Now that I'm able to tell people that I've been interviewed on the show, I'm able to take the recording of that show and leverage it. It gives me more credibility.

**BW:** And that's it. Those of us who deal online quite a bit, we tend to see the world online. We tend to forget or downplay the effect of all the other media out there. Again my background is journalism, and print media are still very, very important, very influential, and that's what we're looking -- influence.

**MR:** Right, and we hear a lot of talk about social influence and social acuity and credibility amongst search engines. Now people cannot hide, because everything will come out and blah blah.

You know, I want to give people a little bit more about you. You've done radio, you've done TV journalism, and you used to do interviews of... I remember seeing a video that you showed me of a martial artist, correct?

**BW:** Yes. In the Eighties and Nineties I had a regular feature segment on a nationally syndicated TV show about martial arts, *The Martial Arts World*.

**MR:** And what is your ranking, if you don't mind me asking? I know you don't like to brag but a lot of people ought to know that Brother Brian is no joke when it comes to his professional journalism and radio and TV experience and also his martial arts experience.

**BW:** *Seishiryu Sogobudo, yondan des'*... I'm a fourth degree black belt Seishiryu.

**MR:** Ain't no joke, Brother Brian? If anybody ever wants to mess with me, I'm going to hook up with Brother Brian in Kentucky and then we'll go from there. Brother Brian, you actually headed out to Kentucky, now right? That you'll be leaving there and heading into another area...

**BW:** Yeah. I'm going into one state north in September. Not a huge distance but I'm going into another geographic area, yes.

**MR:** The reason I bring that up is because you could do what you do anywhere because your work is with you. Your sound booth, your studio or whatever, you've created what you are. That's the beauty of doing what you're doing. While we're talking about **Stroking The Media**, which leads me into this first question and you could touch on-- the fact that you are able to do what you do anywhere. I'm going to ask you this question as well. What's the difference between your **Stroking The Media** product or **Stroking The Media** approach and so many self promotion or public relations systems out there?

**BW:** The big difference is that I actually come from a journalistic background. I got started in the news business back during the lead up to the Watergate scandal and through the Watergate scandal, and I continued in daily journalism until about 1982. I've been in quite a few markets. I then was a sort of a guest correspondent editorialist, Op Ed page writer. I've actually been a regional newspaper editor. I've done a lot of work. Well, in fact, we mentioned the martial arts background; I was contributing editor for both **Inside Karate** and **Inside Kung Fu** magazines. They're printed out in Burbank out in your area. Also for **Black Belt** magazine, I've done a lot of work for them. So I've had experience in pretty much every aspect of the news and communications media. So when the Internet came along, I saw it for what it was - another slice of the pie. Now unfortunately, so many people focus *only* on that slice of the pie these days and only on what can be done in an automated fashion, they forget all of the things we used to do before we had Internet. I call myself a "news dinosaur".

Let me ask, Mark, did you ever see the movie, **"All the President's Men"**?

**MR:** You know, I did, but it was so long ago...

**BW:** Let me tell you, if you get the chance, watch it again. It is such a time capsule because it was only done about a year after President Nixon resigned. And what you had going on there was, you had two street reporters from the **Washington Post** who happened onto the story. They connected the dots, they became major national figures, and they show in that movie the type journalism we used to do. Today, you have to explain "What is that thing they're standing in?" "Oh, it's called a phone booth, dear. That's what we used to have before we had cell phones." And they're going through piles and piles and piles of library cards and physical paper notes at the Library of Congress and I say "That's what we had before we had personal computers and databases. We actually went through papers."

I put **Stroking The Media** that category. It's an old low-tech approach, but the underlying principles are the same, and it's about getting to the right people who will then recognize you as an authority in your field and come to rely on you, and it has to do with understanding the nature of the news business. That's it. This is not a method of advertising. It's not a way to get paid advertising. It's not a way to place ads or solo ads or anything like that. It's a way to get the news media, first of all in your area and then radiating out from your area, to consider you as a credible, reliable news source on a repeated basis, so that when you have an idea for a story, they take you seriously.

**MR:** So it's almost like releasing a press release and getting picked up locally from the local newspapers, to eventually maybe a national paper picking up the story, and the next thing you know, you end up on **"Good Morning America"**?

**BW:** Well, that's part of it, but it's also about developing long-term relationships, not just sending press releases. I used to be one of the people, I was a news director at two stations, and I was an anchor at several, I was the person who received those press releases and sifted through them.

**MR:** I don't mean to cut you off, but I know what you're talking about, because we have a real estate agent out here who's formed a really good relationship with an NBC reporter who does these Sunday afternoons, you know, live. And he also comes to the restaurants and saying and he does like... and he eats at the restaurant and kind of gives them a review. He's also shot some of the real estate commercial, if he will, for this real estate agent. So he's able to get this guy from LA all the way to the Inland Empire. So I wanted to point this out before people kind of a pass over it, what you said was very, very important is about establishing or developing that relationship with these centers of influence in radio media.

**BW:** Not just radio, no. Let me correct you there. Television, radio, newspapers, magazines, the whole spectrum. We talked about radio a lot because that is my principal background when news radio was actually a force, the last decade or so in which news radio was an important segment of the news business. Today, it's pretty well gone. So, we don't want to think only in terms of radio. We really want to think in terms of various print media and reach from there.

Let me give you an important reason why. The difference between having yourself cited as an authority, regarded an authority in print as opposed to doing broadcast, is you've got something in your hand that you can copy and send out to people much more easily than you can a video file or an audio file.

**MR:** That's where I'm going to beg to differ because I always tell people to get things on video. Because you can transcribe them, you can chop them up, you can then have a print version. I can always tell people, when you get your testimonials, it's great to get them emailed to you, but try to give video because you can refurbish video in three different ways.

**BW:** That's right, if you're having testimonials submitted to you. Here I'm talking about being mentioned and quoted in news media by someone else.

**MR:** There is so much to cover in this bonus report. I want to go ahead and jump in here. We already talked about what qualifies you to teach these tactics so I'm not going to ask you that because you've given us a lot of your background. I know that we could go on, because you and I talked about some political things and conspiracy things in the past. Not to mention your Native American spiritual background, impressive background. A lot of people don't know you like I do. But why do you feel that we have return or we should be returning to pre-Internet methods?

**BW:** For one reason, simply because the Internet is fragile. I just went through something in the last few days. I'm with one of the biggest Internet service providers out here. I was just down for 18 hours because somebody took a backhoe through one of their cables. Two weeks ago, I was down for a day. Last month, I was down for three days. So, the Internet is great. It's wonderful. But it's fragile. We tend to overlook the print media. And the print media, in the mind of other journalists, is still the most influential, with television following closely behind. What happens when you have people doing this blast of news releases to people they don't know is, you're just a stranger. It's like when you submit a book manuscript the way we used to call "over-the-transom" or a "slush pile" manuscript; you're nobody, you get someone to look at the first paragraph, and usually it gets canned. What you have to do is gradually develop a relationship, and I have some tools in there where we go into some of my other background, we won't talk about it in any detail. It has to do with intelligence gathering.

**MR:** I know some of that side of you. We will keep a lid on it though. So, for those of you who are listening to this, because you guys picked this up as a bonus to **Stroking The Media**, so make sure you delved into that because you find out a lot more and some other methods that Brother Brian has talked about with regards to being able to leverage this method. In the course, in this package, you seemed to advise the promoter to spy on the potential media contact. Is that ethical Brother Brian?

**BW:** We like to use the term spying. I like to use some terminology out of the intelligence game for what we're doing. But honestly, I'm not saying to invade their privacy. I'm saying to gradually find out what you can. For example, if I talked to you for a while, I'll find out what school you went to. I'll find out where you're really from. I'll find out how many people in your family. Now you and I have been talking over a couple of years, I could put together a reasonable dossier on you right now. If I really look at all these different factors in the tool that I provide in here, I'll know a lot more about you. Now, we're not saying to use any unethical means. As you learn things about somebody and their background which would come up in different ways... conversation, some bio. If you haven't met or you don't know that journalist yet, they'll sometimes give you clues in their news stories. You simply accumulate these. You have these clues, you put them in a particular place. You'll know that person a little bit better, you can speak to them a little better because you've actually taken the time to learn something about their life. It's not just another email address on list that you sent thousands copies of your press release to.

**MR:** So it is sort of like doing comparative analysis on competition?

**BW:** Absolutely. And it's like seeing what this person is really interested in, and why spend your time if this person's interest is really the financial industry, and what's going on in the financial regulation? Why are you going to bother coming to them with an idea about a new approach to batting practice? That's not the person you need to talk to. **Unless,** you've done your homework. You find out that they were on their college softball team and his real goal was to be a pro player. Then you've got your foot in the door with them, and have them recommend the story to somebody else. Now, it's not some stranger (you) coming off the street talking to their sports reporter. It's their financial editor talking to their sports reporter. It's one of the family, one of the fraternity, recommending you.

**MR:** That's a great way to put it. It's one of the fraternity, one of their own members. It's almost like a concept that I had put on a while ago called "Zero to Hero" concept where you borrow someone else's credibility. For example, the Offline Gold training. When you're trying to do business with people, they don't know you; they're going to listen to their bank managers, their CPAs who they have a relationship with, because that person is recommending you. So kind of go from a "zero to hero" because they are lending that credibility to you.

**BW:** Exactly. And what is also going to happen, if you have a small group of journalists... the journalistic business is not that big anymore; in fact, it's constantly downsizing. What's going to happen is if you have really good credibility, you've done really good face time with somebody, when you have an idea and it's not right for them, they will say "Hey, but I know somebody over at this publication that it's good for." They'll recommend you and pretty soon, you've got a big network going of people who think of you. What you really want is if anything occurs in your field, you are the first person they think of to get a quote. You are the first person they think of to come to when they're having a slow news day. "Good Ol' Mark is usually good on some kind of feature story I can run when there's nothing happening. Let me call him and see if he has anything on top of his head."

**MR:** Right! That brings me to my next question because this is kind of cause a lot of people to hold back. A lot of people will have that fear, if you will, or that feeling of saying "Am I good enough?" or what have you because your approach is based on presenting the promoter as an expert authority. And I know my answer to this question but I want our listeners to hear it from you because this is your brain child. Will that be realistic for most readers?

**BW:** Everybody is an authority about something. The question is, is it something anyone else is interested in? My response to that is you better actually know what you are talking about before you go deal with a real journalist, because they *will* ask you follow-up questions. So have your stuff together before you even start this. Have your stuff together. But then again, how do you get to be an authority? By knowing a little more than the next person.

**MR:** That's my biggest pet peeve, Brother Brian, with my students, and I hate to jump in here, but it's a valid point that we have to make sure people are aware of. I tell my students most of the time, when you guys don't close your Offline Gold deals, it's because you were not confident enough in knowing your product or service. You have to know your product or service inside and out so when that these people ask questions about mobile marketing, mobile sms/text messaging, mobile apps, social media, whatever, you not only have to be able to answer it, but answer it with confidence. **Stroking The Media** is going to help them, in a sense, realize that they are an expert in something and how do they proceed from there, Brother Brian?

**BW:** That's it. You have to know your stuff. You have to have your facts straight. And you have to be completely honest, completely ethical because you only get one chance to blow that with any real journalist.

There are just so many ways of reaching out. One thing people don't understand, people who haven't been in the news media, don't understand how much pressure, how much deadline pressure there is. I used to work for an all-news station and we had three newscasts per hour. Three newscasts, three 20-minute newscasts per hour to fill with different content. We couldn't use the same content. It was just a constant deadline pressure, constant demand for new information. Now, that was back before we had all of these cable networks, all of these Internet outlets, there's a huge demand for news content out there. You don't have to be the world's greatest expert, you just have to have good, solid information about something reasonably newsworthy. And we go into that, how to tell if something is newsworthy or not. Then you make your connections with people and you present it.

Now, let me give you an example on one incident where doing research helped me. I was doing some public relations work for the Native American center here in West Kentucky. They were having a performer who has a big national reputation -- at least within the Native American community -- to do a fundraising concert. The local weekly newspaper wasn't interested in doing an advance story on it. We wanted, of course, an advance story to pique the ticket sales before the event, not just a celebrity story after the fact. So they weren't interested. However, because of my contacts with that editor and with the editor at another larger regional newspaper, I knew they both needed a Wednesday publication date. So what I did was I went to the other newspaper and I offered the same story. They were interested because they had a greater content need. Once they agreed to do the story, and I set them up with the interview by phone. I then went back to the first local weekly, because I knew they had a big bug (about the second paper). One of their big peeves was they were never going to be beaten by this other newspaper on something that was happening in their own local area.

**MR:** that is a big issue with reporters. They don't want to be "scooped", they call it.

**BW:** They don't want to be scooped in their home beat. They don't want to be scooped in their home beat by an outsider. And I went back and I just very innocently said "Oh. That's alright. Don't worry about that. Thank you for your time and consideration. But I've already placed the story and the interview with your competition over here." I didn't say it quite that way. I said the big paper by name, and they're going to do an interview with the entertainer. And in ten minutes, the small local called me back and they wanted the interview, too, so they could get the press on the same day with it and not be beaten on their home turf by an outsider. So I placed two feature stories for my client, right? That's the way it is. But again, I couldn't have done it that way it I hadn't been on a first name basis with both of those editors and known what their competitive relationship, what their rivalry was. That's the information you need to gather, and you don't do it overnight, and you don't do it by any kind of unethical or invasive means. You do it by old-style information gathering.

**MR:** You said something that again I need to point out in case people missed it. You said you have to make sure that is newsworthy.

**BW:** That's it. We both receive a number of press releases and you look at it and you go "that's interesting, and I'm glad you're improving your widget. You now have 15% more efficient widget, and outside of the business page, does anyone care?" Now, if you're doing a story about an upgrade on your project, you have nowhere to send it. If you are doing a somewhat pedestrian business-related story, a story related to your business -- and I give you a number of ideas in this book of things where you can take almost nothing and turn it into a story -- it'll be a story for the business page, not for the front section. That's where you really have to look at something. What are the biggest stories top of your mind without really thinking, just emotional reaction, Mark? Top stories of last week.

**MR:** For me, well of course the Colorado Shooting, God forbid. God bless those...

**BW:** Colorado?

**MR:** Yes.

**BW:** What else?

**MR:** Top of the story this week. Well here, locally, there's been a couple of cops busted for doing some unscrupulous things here locally. Right now, I'm drawing a blank; this is too early in the morning.

**BW:** Cops, cops and the Olympics opened yesterday, okay?

**MR:** You know I watched the Olympics opening ceremony last night and I was half asleep so I apologize.

**BW:** That's cool but like I said, I'm not that big into sports either. But some people are. So the real question is, do you have, in your official capacity, anything to say about any of those things?

**MR:** Okay. There's something that I was going to bring up because my mind just hit this like "Oh my God. I've got to share this with Brother Brian." We're going to be quoted in this recording, but I've got your next follow up product. I know that you are not doing this for the money Brother Brian. A lot of people think that this is all about how you... the only way you can make money... this is not what we are doing here. We really do want to get information out for people to leverage it. It has to be newsworthy, it has to be eye-catching so I'm going to share with you right now... I'm really quoted over here. The next product for you, and I'm going to ask you right now is to put something together to teach people how to expand more on the topic of newsworthiness. This is basically what I'm saying. So we're going to work on that because there's a lot of the online tools that'll help you do that. One of the examples that I can't show here is using Google Trends to leverage on what are the top stories right now trending on Google. There's a lot of other tools and a lot other stuff that we can get in to. So that's going to be the next thing you and I are going to team up on. We're going to talk on how they can make themselves newsworthy.

**BW:** Let me ask you for example. When, God bless her, Oprah was still doing her show, she used to have a page online, you could go and you could see who her guests were several weeks in advance. If you knew she got somebody coming on talking about sexual assault and sexual assault defense training, and you know that's coming up in two week, if you're running a martial arts school, if you're running a self-defense course, you got that long to have your story in the hands of your local and regional news media as an advance story. You say "this is being featured on Oprah on x date", so your paper might want to do it the same date or the next day... or even a day or two ahead to make it look like Oprah is getting story ideas from you!

**MR:** Brother Brian, we did that with affiliate marketing and I'm going to give you two examples...

**BW:** But first you have to promise the audience this wasn't just a set-up!

**MR:** No. You know honestly, as God as my witness, it wasn't. The fact that you just said that, my mind went straight to these two examples that we did that. You might remember me saying this with the Internet marketing coach back in the day. It was two examples where we leveraged Oprah. We used to do that. A lot of the IMers used to say you can't make money watching TV. You got to do this. You got to do that. I used to be the opposite. I'm always been the type to go against the flow. I used to purposely watch Oprah and I used to tell people to watch Oprah. In modern times now, I would say watched **"The View"**, and watch this other talk shows that have these interesting stories out there. Two quick examples. One of them was Jibbitz for crocs. Do you know what Jibbitz are?

**BW:** No, I don't.

**MR:** Jibbitz was an idea that came from this mother who... you know what Crocs are, right? They look like clogs with holes in it. There was this mother who thought that the little girl, her daughter wanted to spice up her little shoes. So what she did was she took earrings and she put them basically at the top so that the back of the earring would pop through the hole. And then she kind of trimmed that metal piece that went into the earring so that it wouldn't poke her feet. She put some kind of backing things on there and started decorating these shoes with earrings. And so other parents would see daughter's crocs and ask "Oh, where'd you get those at? Can you hook me up with it? Can you make some for me?" So she started making these for other people and selling them. Now she's become a multi-millionaire. Well, she was on Oprah and her company was valued over 15 million dollars and she stated this line called Jibbitz. Now Jibbitz is licensing Disney, licensing you name the cartoon, you name the... Angry Birds, you name it and Jibbitz has these things out there. I knew had a date and time that she was going to be on Oprah, we threw up a bunch of affiliate sites trying to sell Jibbitz and everything from Amazon, you name it. So that was one story. To take it even further back, we had been promoting one of the original launches of "The Secret." When we found out Oprah was going to have some of these speakers from "The Secret" on her show, we went up and started throwing affiliate sites around selling the DVD for "The Secret" and selling the courses that some of these speakers were releasing as affiliates, and we made a ton of money doing it. So it's a hundred percent hitting the nail on the head that when you know of something ahead of time.

That's one of the cool things about Google Trends is you could find out what's trending. In this next product that I'm going to hold you to that I'm going to keep you to... I'm going to keep bugging you about, Brother Brian. We got to show them not only how to become newsworthy but where to scoop everybody else. It's almost like stock market, right? It's almost like watching the pits. You need to know when to get in and when to get out of stock or we want to know when is the jump off point to get to that story before everybody else. because that can make this individual a celebrity.

See, an example is back in 2007-2008 when I was talking to local chambers of commerce about Twitter and this and that, when people weren't listening, "you guys got to get involved with this stuff, Twitter and Facebook. They're going to be really big." everyone was all about MySpace. I was telling them "you guys got to do it." And a year later I come back to them and "how many of you guys created a Twitter account yet?" they're not doing it yet. A year later. Another year goes by, now that news stations, everybody has a twitter account when they're watching their TV news. That's when they decided to do it, because everybody else was doing it. But that's not when you want to do it, right?

We want to be ahead of the curve. We want to be ahead of the wave because that's the people that make the most amount of money or get the most attention. It's not about riding the wave in. It's about being the first on that wave. It's like a surf competition. That person that gets out there and gets on the waves the most and cuts, does all these things on the wave, everybody else is trying to swim out to catch the wave. And you want to be on the beach. You want to be relaxing with a Mai Tai.

**BW:** Yeah. Absolutely. And again, it so much boils down to its combination of **what you know** and **who you know** and **how well you tell who you know what you know**.

**MR:** That brings me up to something we both mentioned here, about online press releases. You don't seem to be a big fan of the online press release services. Why do you advise promoters to do it themselves?

**BW:** I wouldn't say I'm not a big fan of them. I'm not a big fan of them using them *exclusively,* and there are several reasons. One is, they're expensive. They're good for what you get, but it's shotgun. You're just kind of scatter-gunning your approach and again, we get back to my point: you're sending them to strangers. I would rather send 10 or 20 people that I know a release... 10 or 20 people who already know that I am a reliable source and are likely either to use it or to refer it to someone else, because from that publication or appearance, in whatever media that appears, that will spawn other stories, because **journalists watch each other constantly.**

I did a language class on the other end of the state teaching Cherokee, and there was a little story in the weekly paper that ran there, and that kicked off 5 or 6 other stories across the state, across the Ohio Valley, just because there was nobody else teaching the language anymore. You don't want to throw out all these great services like PR Web, they're wonderful and Vocus and Cision. But at the same time, they're pretty pricey. I'm a big fan of use-the-free-tools-first, and your free tool is your own email, and we get into how you put a news release together so that it's going to be noticed and it's going to get to the person that it needs to get to.

Here's one thing that I do differently than a lot of the other gurus writing on this, and some of them are friends, but my background is broadcast news. As we've been talking longer and my voice starts coming back to me here this morning. I probably *sound* like my background is broadcast news. But there's a difference between writing something that is to be read and writing something that is to be spoken. You better not have any tongue twisters in there. And if you can write something that can be, as we say, "read cold" -- in other words, a bulletin comes in, somebody runs in from the side of the camera, hands a piece of paper to the anchorman, and he reads it after barely looking at it. That's reading something "cold". And I just dated myself because I said "hands him a piece of paper" instead of "throws it up on the teleprompter". But I never used a teleprompter, we didn't have them yet! But the thing is, it has to be written in a certain style, and the only way you can do that is to write it, to speak it, to listen to it. If you can do that, that is natural speech. Even if you then take that into print, it looks so much better than what's written by a lot of the people who are using these press release tools or writing on -- sorry, they're writing about garbage, and some of them writing about something that nobody really cares about.

When it gets to a journalist or editor, you want that person to at least look through the first paragraph before he or she pitches it. Preferably, you want them to think it's a good story, even if not for now. It's something I'm going to sandbag for a slow news day.

**MR:** A really neat way for people to learn something, I think. Here's going to be a freebie that I'm going to give everybody. So when they talk about... when people say "okay, you know this audio bonus..." I want them to feel that it's worth listening to. Because we are well over the 30-minute mark right now.

But something that I do, and I watch a lot of TV, Brother Brian, you know that. Something that I like paying attention to is, because we're talking about pitching stories right now, you just mentioned. I'm going to come back to the point you made about the teleprompter in a minute, but it's TMZ. I love watching TMZ, **"30 Mile Zone".** They like to scoop all these celebrity stories from all of these papers and like to be the ones to break the story. They do a lot of that, especially right now what's in the story is like Michael Jackson's family, they're all fighting, Michael Jackson's mother was missing and now reportedly they found her in Arizona and they brought her back to California. The custody has been taken away from her blah blah blah. the point I'm making is that when you watch TMZ and now they have gone to a TMZ live. They have a recorded version and then at 3pm my time, they have the live version. You get to watch them pitch their stories to Harvey Levin. So Harvey Levin will write them up on this board and they all pitch they're stories. It's funny because some of the stories, they crack jokes on like this one guy as talking about a dream where he had Kim Kardashian appear on his dream. So one of the other guys started, "Oh, are we pitching stories now?" So you get to learn and see even these people they have really good stories with celebrities a lot of their stories don't make the cut for TMZ. Not only do you get to watch the recorded version and learn how these people position and pitch their stories about these celebrities. Two different people will pitch their stories in a different way in a different format, what interests them. But then when you watch the live version, see the breaking news as its coming through. And they actually hit almost everybody in the news office for TMZ has the webcam at their desk so you actually see them. They all do same thing, they all do research online. They're all researching it online. They have their field reporters but they're all researching the story online and then they're pitching it to Harvey Levin to try to make the show.

**BW:** It's a great resource.

**MR:** That happens every day, though, and at the news desk. Every night, everybody's pitching in the morning, what stories, or the day before, what stories are we going to do. It happens with TV as well. What are we going to roll with? What are our breaking news going to be today?

**BW:** Sure because. One thing... again, the news media shrinks somewhat as far as the number of real outlets there that are originating the stories. It's very competitive. You have to be able to assign your resources. You have a smaller staff. You have to be able to assign those resources, those staffers to what they are able to get the most result. There're just some legendary stories about it but you can't spend a lot of time researching something that may not be much of a story. Back thirty years ago, "60 Minutes" would let people have as much as six months to develop and double-check and triple-check stories and sources to produce a piece. It was more usually about one month. I usually had to have it the next day!

**MR:** It's interesting that you are bringing this up. I saw a documentary, not so much a documentary but a recording of a panel just a couple weeks ago on the biggest Current TV. It's another channel I like to watch.

They were talking about the role of the journalist today with social media. That pretty much makes almost everybody a reporter. Not like someone who's been trained on how to write but anybody now can whip out their phone and take pictures or video like what's going on in Syria today, and upload it to YouTube or upload it to Twitter and be the breaking story. They just broke the story. With the beatings of this young gentleman that was killed here in Loma Linda, California by the cops. People had their phones and they were recording this stuff. So they in essence become the people that break the news stories, right? This documentary or this panel was talking about, what is *our* role now? How does the journalist remain being journalist, or how do they keep their job, and how do they continue to try to get paid because now, they can be scooped by people with a cell phone and Twitter and Facebook, because people are blogging this or Facebooking the story or Twittering the story?

**BW:** Again, It goes back to what I said; the news media, the news professionals are under a lot of pressure. Now they have to compete with somebody Tahrir Square in Cairo with a cellphone. How do you do that? You do that by having background. You do that by being able to do analysis. And being able to evaluate whatever you're being sent, whatever is being sent to YouTube or Twitter. You do it with more and more background but there's more pressure. So what I teach, the approach that I use in **Stroking The Media** is how to become the journalist's best friend, somebody who understands where they're coming from. Pretty much you must become a journalist, if you hadn't been one already, to understand what's going on in their minds what their pressures are. You're no longer somebody in front of them handing them or pitching them a product or a story. You're now somebody who has their back.

**MR:** So I want to be very clear... everything that they need is within this package, **Stroking The Media**? The only reason I talk about that, I'm going to try and press you to try to expand on one of the areas, on one of the topics which is being newsworthy is because I think we could spend a lot more time to talk about other tools and things and spend more time with you, the expert, in getting some of that information out and evaluating it, because your time is very valuable, and I want to say again, thank you for allowing us to do this interview, this bonus interview. I really appreciate it.

**BW:** Let me give you just one more piece. This is something that we talked a lot about our areas of expertise, and we know that we're going to pitch the things that will make us money. we have to understand that. But sometimes, you will get contacts from a completely different area and you have to remember to be an upstanding part of the community. in New Jersey, one of the biggest newspaper chains in the country, Gannett News, they're the people who have USA Today. They set up what were effectively race panels in their different outlets. This meant in different parts of the community, they wanted to have a file that they could go to immediately when something happened so they knew who to go to for a comment. They would have somebody, for example, in the Hispanic community, in the black community, in the Italian community, whatever. They would have of list of people who they had already vetted as being legitimate spokespeople for that community. I became their spokesperson for the Native American community, so anytime something happened with a Native American spin to it, anything where that they wanted to get a little more depth, I was the one they called. That led to my being quoted constantly as a news source, which led to many other news contacts and community contacts because nothing exists in a vacuum. Everything today is interconnected.

**MR:** Because you were the authority. you were the expert in that area, that niche. why go to someone else when this is the person that is apparently the voice of that particular demographic?

**BW:** More importantly, I'm the one who was already in their Rolodex. They don't have to ask, "Gee, who do I go to?"

**MR:** Right. they don't have to go looking.

**BW:** You have to maintain your contacts. Strangely enough just because it was exotic, there was somebody who was doing what was being billed as Tibetan something or other, and they asked me for some reason. "This sounds somewhat wrong. We know this isn't your area, but do you know anybody who might be an authority on Tibetan culture, Tibetan Buddhism?" and I said "Yes, I do!" and I hooked them up with Dr. Robert Thurman, probably the leading authority on the East Coast, at Columbia University.

**MR:** So they are leveraging your connections?

**BW:** They're leveraging my connections that they didn't even know I had! They got to the man who is a close associate to the Dalai Lama, so this newspaper was not quoting somebody who just read something on Wikipedia. they were quoting one of the biggest experts in the country. I just gave them the phone number and all the contact information. The guy also happens to be Uma Thurman's father. so...

**MR:** Whoa! that's cool.

**BW:** Right?

**MR:** You're like saying, "I know Uma Thurman's dad. Let me just hook you up with his number."

**BW:** I know Uma's dad, yeah, so let me hook you up. I didn't even mention that connection, because it had nothing to do with their story. If you were wondering why she has that name, "Uma Karuna", Mother of Compassion, is the name of a Tibetan goddess. So it's a question of the people you know, and you don't know who *they* know until you ask.

**MR:** I always tell people, be careful how you treat people, because you never know when you walk in to an office to try to sell your products and services, or to do an interview, or to ask for a press release or a story to make the newspaper, you never know and that person that you treated like dirt is on the other side of that desk.

**BW:** That's the way it is, and at the same time, you never know when that person could do a favor for you, or in the example I just gave where you can do a favor for that person.

**MR:** Now, it's the law of reciprocity kicking in. They owe **you**.

**BW:** They sure do!

**MR:** Now, let me share this with you because you mentioned something earlier about being able to speak right then and there because there weren't teleprompters back in the day. They handed you a paper.

It's very interesting you bringing that up because a week ago yesterday, I attended the first-ever Latino Media Con and Expo. It was held July 20th and 21st in Pasadena at the Pasadena Convention Center and everybody that's anybody, that's involved with Latin media, in TV, film, music, and digital, was there. Brother Brian, you would have loved it!. It was put on by the National Hispanic Coalition. we had people from Univision, NBC Universal, Channel 47-California, Telemundo, Comcast, Mundos , Disney Television Group, The Walt Disney Studios, ESPN, La Opinion, Chevrolet, these were all the sponsors and people that had booths there. CBS Corporation, Fox, Nielsen Ratings were there. It goes on and on and on. NAB, NAB had representation there. Media partners - ABC 7, CBS 2, KCAL9, Fox 11, Latino Broadcasting Company, Latino Style Magazine, Latin Leader Magazine, Universal Film Magazines. I said I can go on and on. And it was really neat because they has topics everything from the A-Z to the Hollywood guilds, creating Hollywood access, empowering Latinos in the entertainment, first look at the new movie coming out called "End of Watch".  They had Latinos in social media and digital media; they had the Excellence In Media awards. So we got to meet a lot of celebrities a lot of "very influential people", and I don't want to say like a god-like power but powerful people in media.

The key note speaker of the day was Haim Saban. I'm not sure if that name rings a bell, but in 1988, he formed the Saban Entertainment Group which was an international television distribution and merchandising company. He merged companies with Rupert Murdoch's Fox Kids Network in 1995 and in 1997 the Saban-Fox partnership acquired the Fox Family Channel, which was then restructured under the Fox Family Worldwide banner. Fox Family Worldwide was sold to The Walt Disney company in October 2001. In 2002, Saban founded the Saban Center for Middle East Policy in Brookings Institution and he currently chairs its international advisory board. What he's gone on to do since then now is focus on Spanish language media. And they acquired Univision Communications Incorporated which is they're huge. they are the premier Spanish language media company.

The reason I'm bringing that up is I got to have an exchange with Saban, Haim Saban, in front of hundreds of people. Check this out. Here's a great example how to become famous.  I went from a zero to hero. Saban was responsible for bringing a little known group. You definitely got to know this because they were martial artists, Brother Brian.  He was famous for bringing the Power Rangers. He owned the whole Power Rangers distribution, the Power Ranger movies and all these stuff and long story short, Saban was being interviewed by one of the most well respected gentlemen in Latin media today, Alex Nogales. They're sitting up there, it's just two sits on the panel, we're all watching this, and he's asking all these really deep in depth questions and he's says "Okay. I think we have some time for some audience questions." I honestly wasn't going to go up there. They have a mic in front of the stage but they had this round table sitting there where we all have lunch. So the first guy goes up and asks these so-called deep questions. Saban had talked about "thank you guys all for supporting the Power Rangers. That made us a lot of money blah blah". So the guy goes up there and he was saying "I just want to thank you. You have been this and that." He's asking some question about the merger and why focusing on the Latin media. so I tell my VP of marketing and sales who was sitting next to me and mind you, it was $175 to get in to this place. That's what they charge for the first ever Latino Mediacon and Expo. So even if you're a nonprofit, it was $150, even if you're a student, it was $125. People that got in there either had to have money or were sponsored by magazine or TV news press pass or whatever.

I wasn't going to go up there but I decided to go up there because I had to share this story. I felt the inspiration to let him know that what he did in bringing the Power Rangers wasn't just entertainment for a lot of us. At that time, Brother Brian, was a very low period in my life. Me and you have shared a lot of things and I'm not ashamed to tell people that I deal a lot of dirt coming up -- former gang banger, did a lot of things that I'm not proud of. And so I had to hustle being a single father. At that time, it was very difficult for me. And I had two boys and I had to raise them. They were still little babies so I had to make a decision at that time in my life... do I go back to hustling and doing dirt or the devil is trying to pull me that way or do I go ahead and try to figure out some other way?

So my aunt had a flower shop and I was working part time for a flower shop. This was about 20 years ago. I used to go pick up the Mylar balloons and helium tanks for her and flower stuff so there was a warehouse in Ontario, California that sold these Mylar balloons and there were these Power Rangers on a stick. They were small. The balloons were about a foot long. They were each character. There were blue, pink green, yellow, white rangers, red rangers. I thought "let me get them wholesale from this lady and then on the weekends, I'm going to go and try to sell these for at least double. Make some money."

So I was buying them for $1.50 and I figured I could sell them for $3-$5 at the park. So I think, just me walking and selling these and I'm going to look like an illegal street vendor. So what can I do to stand out? So I actually went out and bought this green leotard spandex jumpsuit, got these old white boots at the secondhand store... well, they were actually black, we painted them white, got a white wide leather belt, and actually bought a Power Ranger helmet that we had to paint to look like the Green Ranger. So I ended up looking like the Green Power Ranger. Now, I'm at the park in full character costumes selling these things for $5. And I could not get the kids to stop mobbing me. This is God's honest truth. My mom could verify this. I went from just selling these things for $5 thinking I'm making good enough money until somebody approached me at the park the very first day and saying, "will you do my son's birthday party next week?" I didn't know what to charge. She goes, "I'll pay you $75 for an hour to come out." And I said "You got it and we can do a 2-hour minimum." So I started doing parties, for $150 minimum to $300-$500. And people were treating me really good. they would feed me and everything. I would go over there. I had so much fun. It was a period of my life where being that green power ranger had changed my life for that moment for that instant that lead to other things.

The reason I'm bringing up the story is because I had this exchange with Haim Saban, this billionaire. I got up there in front of everybody and said, "I have to share this story with you" and before I could finish the story, he interrupted me and he said "let me ask you one thing" because I told them "thanks for bringing up the Power Rangers." Everybody was kind of clapping, they were giving cheers, like "thank you for bringing up Power Rangers", "I really grew up on that" and he said, "well, let me ask you one thing, did you buy any of the Power Ranger toys?"

I go, "Oh my God yes. I remember having to go to Kmart fighting people for these Power Rangers like..." they were like life-size dolls. There were pillows. People would fight for the colors like the red one, the white one, the blue one, those were the most popular, and I was fighting women... like they were grabbing them like "No I need this one." You know how it is with the Cabbage Patch dolls back in the day. Everybody was grabbing them... So I'm like "No I need this one." They are like pulling on it and I am like "No no no. I've got every other color. I need this for my sons. Let me have this for my sons." And he started laughing and well he started laughing and he makes like... it wasn't really intentional but he kind of almost made like a smart alec remark. He goes "Thank you for putting money in my family's pocket."

Everybody kind of started laughing like and I go "No sir. You got it twisted. Thank YOU for putting money in my family's pocket." That's when I told him what I did. I said "because of you, because of the Power Rangers..." I went ahead and I told them the whole story about the Mylar balloons, about these costumes, puts this together this costume and dressed like the Power Ranger, started charging like $75 an hour. and he just looked at me and then Alex was like "Can you imagine the creativeness of this guy?" And I said "Thank you, because in that period of my life where I had to make a decision do I go back to my street knowledge and the street hustling and the gang banging and the dirt, or do I do something creative and try to stand out and make money legitimately? And because of you, I was able to make thousands of dollars and able to feed my family and pay my rent and do what I have to do but I had to stop that at one point."

And he said "why?" I said "It wasn't because I thought I was going to be sued for copyright infringement." Everybody started laughing Again, I said, "It was because I gained too much weight and instead of looking like the Green Power Ranger, I looked like the Green Burrito!"

And everybody started laughing again.

The reason that I have to share this story with you, Brother Brian, is because it relates to what we talked about today in this bonus session. The rest of the day, every booth I went to, walking down every aisle, I was known as the "Hey! You're the Green Ranger," "You're that guy", "You're the Green Burrito", "It was great how you expanded on Haim and made money off of him.", "It was awesome that you made money off of him."

So it was almost like a taste of celebrity if for half of that day which I thought was really cool.

Now that wasn't my intention. But now because I had that, I felt a little bit more confident walking in there. You know there are people, big time people in media. Who do I know in NBC Universal that I could...? Well now, they knew **me!** People were coming up to me. I felt the sense of being confident.

Guess what I walked out of there with?

**BW:** Shakira?

**MR:** I wish! She wasn't there. But there were a lot of other celebrities. But that brings us to a point in the teleprompter. At one point before all this happened. You had Laura Diaz from Channel 7 who was now on Channel 9 news and Big Boy who was a very, very well known radio personality. They were introducing all these people and they were getting on stage and receiving awards and all the teleprompter broke at one point. And they both froze. You could see the panic in their faces. They were kind of "Oh well. Our teleprompter just gone out so I guess we got to kill time today and bring this back up. I guess what we're suppose to do is introduce the next award recipient." And you could tell they hadn't read their cue cards because they were depending on their teleprompter. They had to wait for it to come back. So I thought, that it's interesting that you say you have to be able to know and talk right away and be well informed and researched. So what I ended up walking out of the Latino Media Con and Expo with was some contacts. What have you been talking about this whole time?

**BW:** Not *some* contacts. You walked out with *a lot* of contacts. More importantly, contacts who saw you as somebody credible.

**MR:** You're right. I have a stack of cards here. I have a lot of them. But what I'm saying is some contacts. I walked out with some contacts that want to work with me. One of them, the name is Pepe Serna. Now, Pepe Serna may ring a bell to a lot of people. But if you've ever watched the movie **"Scarface"**, Pepe Serna was Angel Fernandez in the movie and it's a very climactic and you'll never forget this moment in **"Scarface"**. He was Tony Montana's friend that was captured by the Colombians and thrown in the bathtub and chained up. He was cut up with a chainsaw. That's who I got to meet. Pepe Serna who was an actor who was in **"Scarface",** and we sat and talk for almost an hour. Next thing you know, he says, "We need to work together. I need a website for this. I've got this project and I have that project. I want to work with somebody who could understand me, who knows my history, who knows my culture who has a hunger and zeal like you, who has knowledge like you."

So he gave me some DVDs to look at and he says "This is what I want you to promote. I've got artwork, I've got this, and I've got that" He's going to end up being one of my clients and promoting me with other people. He's a very awesome guy and I told them "I don't work for free. Just because you're in a big movie like **"Scarface",** there's got to be skin in the game." He says, "No. I'm going to pay you. there's no question. I'm going to pay you." I said "Alright then. As long as you understand that. we could work together." He's already called me since Latin Mediacon.

I hooked up with another person, a lady who owns a production company and I went to the Internet Movie Data Base (IMDB) Online because what do you say, Brother Brian? "Do your research." I went to search to see if she was who she said she was. A Hollywood producer with this company who put out movies. She's actually got the credits in the IMDB. She's got a legitimate production company. She wants to get the word out about a mobile app she's produced and a bunch of other projects she's working on. She wants to do so some crowd funding which is, you know part of one of the services that we offer. She wants somebody who can manage her social media. The main thing is she wants somebody to get the word out about herself and her business. So we've got an appointment this Wednesday in Westwood and she said "if all goes well, I'm going to start and introduce you to all of my Hollywood contacts and friends in the business." She says "I know a lot of celebrities that can use your services."

So again, going to an event like this and hooking up. It just takes like this one, doesn't it, Brother Brian? It just takes one contact, one relationship, one story to break to put you out there.


**BW:** One person who opens the door for you to the others, and one thing where you fall completely into what I'm saying with this approach, this **Stroking The Media** approach is you now have a lot of contacts in the media, in the news media, so that when you do have something and you can put a newsworthy spin on it, they know you, you are already a known source, you are a known quantity, credible source, you can email them. Pick up a phone, whatever, give them a release. As opposed to going to **PR News**, **PR Web**, **Vocus** and blasting it out to a hundred thousand sources and hoping one of them takes it.

**MR:** And the best part of this is they are all going to remember me because I'm going to say "Remember? I'm the guy that told the Green Ranger story."

**BW:** "I'm the Green Burrito"

**MR:** Check it out, Brother Brian. It's been really awesome. You shared a lot of valuable content. I know you're time is valuable. We've been trying to get together or put this thing together. I've been busy. you've been busy. I know that you definitely wanted to over deliver on this package and what this audio bonus interview, you've definitely done that.

Are there any last remaining take aways, any last bit of advice the you give people so that they can take this information, take this package and then make the most of it? Because I know a lot of them are going to be afraid to even take that step and it's always just about getting started. Is there something that you have that would help people? I believe you and I talked about that there's somewhere where people can actually book an hour of your time whether it's to be able to do a Q-and-A with you or I don't' know what you plan to do with them in an hour. But I know it's to help them to develop either their story, their pitch, polish it up or whatever. You were talking about wanting to give people an hour and I know that you're rate is when you do this TV... because I know you're still doing TV ads, TV commercials. I know you were doing at one point; you were doing something for a local radio station for one of the cities in your town. So I know, you're still getting booked, I now you're still getting money and you've got that booming voice for radio. You had something we were talking about. So first thing the takeaways and then, let's talk about what you were thinking of doing for these folks?

**BW:** As takeaways, what I want people to take away from this is the way you get in with the news media is to think like a reporter. You practically have to be one. You become their 'fraternity brother' is what you become. You become the person who has their back. I'm not going to tell you it's immediate; that's not easy. You have to understand the nature of the business, nature of journalism. The main nature of journalism is you better have your facts straight. You better be honest, because once you're credibility is blown, you're done. It's almost impossible to recover. So, get it right. It's good to be fast, it's good to be first. It's better to be correct.

After that, be, legitimately, their friend. Learn about them. Assemble the dossier with the forms that I give you. Assemble the information so that you can talk with them. If you find out that the guy went to Michigan State, don't pretend you went to Michigan State. Just somehow work it in to your follow up questions with him something about Michigan State. Then you actually have to develop rapport. There was a book about 20 years ago called "Instant Rapport". There's no such thing as instant rapport, it takes time. It has to be genuine. Be genuine. The first time I ever saw you, Mark, I still remember. I remember because you had a video and you were sitting there with a briefcase full of cash while all the other gurus were driving around in the cars you knew damn well they rented for the shoot. The way you talked and the way you came on... because I've been through some of that myself. I've worked in very urban settings. I've been in very rural settings most people can't even imagine. I caught my first bullet when I was 15. So it's not fun. I've had a rough life. I looked at you and I said "This guy is either the realist guy I've seen or he's a damn good actor. Either way, I want to know more about what he's saying."

So what I have to say... what I get that whole long thing about journalism, it boils down to one expression. Keep it real.

**MR:** Don't I always say that, Brother Brian?

**BW:** Keep it real.

**MR:** People always say that "what do you mean by keeping it real? I'm always keeping it real." I'm like "you're *not* keeping it real." I love that you said that. I love that you're takeaways are right to the gut. Right now, you are like, you are gut-checking everybody. If you haven't already gone through, going through that dossier and filling it out and doing all these other things that Brother Brian is telling you, and he's a thousand percent correct. I was one of the first people to put up $50,000 in cash and showed that people this is real money that we're doing, and people started swiping my videos and using it to promote their products and services ad giveaways which was really funny to me. So that's when I had to start watermarking everything. But you are right. Before the social media blew up to what it was, even then I always had to keep it real because I never wanted somebody to come up to me later and meet me at a seminar and workshop and say "Oh. You're that BSer." "You're that guy this..." I'm going to tell you a hundred percent. I'm going to keep it real. The new term is "I'm going to keep it 100." That's the new term.

**BW:** Let me tell you something, here's the difference. You can tell a cop you are not holding any weed and you might get by with a bluff. Don't try it with a sniffer dog. And when you're dealing with the news media, you're dealing with the trained sniffer dogs. You better not be holding anything back. You better not be concealing something. It will be spotted very quickly, so quickly that it will make your head spin.

**MR:** Not only spotted, Brother Brian, but then you'll be put on blacklist. Perfect case in point, Oprah. The guy that talked about his life broken into a million pieces. He wrote this book. Oprah had him on her book club, made him famous. He made all these sales with the book and then she comes to find out later, which she admitted was her poor team's fault, they didn't do their research, she came to find out the guy lied about a lot of that. So then he comes back on Oprah and he asked and admits that he lied and then "why did you lie? why did you feel the need to lie?"

**BW:** I'm sure it made him feel third grade again to have Oprah go all like "tell the class why you lied."

**MR:** He went from famous to infamous, right?

**BW:** Exactly. And did he get a job in journalism again?

**MR:** No. No one's ever going to want to publish his books anymore because even the publisher caught heat for that.

**BW:** The same things happen for journalists.

**MR:** The same thing happens in IM. If you're in Internet marketing, your offline goal consultant and you're lying because a lot of the IMers will tell you "Fake it until you make it." Look, I always tell my students, just know what the hell you are talking about. If you could at least talk the game and just really know the product, you could always outsource the development. You can always outsource the marketing piece or the social media management, but know what you are talking about.

**BW:** Know what you are talking about. Absolutely.

**MR:** Bringing this back, full circle Brother Brian. For the folks that picked up this package and are reviewing this bonus interview that we're doing, you have something that you wanted to offer them that I think is really phenomenal and just can't be beat, and that is your time. I know that your time is very valuable which is $200 to $500. When you're doing international consulting, I know that you charge a lot more than that. So what is it exactly that these folks can get from you for picking up this package and what is the preferred friendly family rate that you are going to give it to everybody that is listening to this bonus interview?

**BW:** Honestly, Mark, for people who have come to me as a result of your efforts and as a result of your endorsement, because you are actually endorsing me to your people, I'm going to give them my friend- of-a-friend discount rate of $97 an hour for my time. Usually what I do is that I get on the phone with them, Skype or phone, and we go over whatever it is they need to put the pieces together, and I even go beyond that into whatever they need to really focus in and organize their thoughts about their business and how to present their business and how to use all of the tools. Not just **Stroking The Media** but primarily **Stroking The Media** because they're going to be following up on this package. But there is so much out there that people don't realize is just beyond their fingertips as far as where they're reaching. They don't even know that it's there. There are so many tools out there that we can help anybody who has a clear idea and a newsworthy idea and a newsworthy product. We can help them get local exposure almost immediately, regional exposure, and even national.

**MR:** So you are going to help them raise their target hone it in?

**BW:** Absolutely. That's what it is about. It's about developing the contact. It's about being focused. The first thing that people don't want, if you're a journalist and you're receiving hundreds of these propositions each day, you don't want to guess what it is about. I've seen so many people who tried to be mysterious. They tried to do a sales letter where they're using some sort of mystery or confusion aspect in their subject line on the email. That's not the place for it. It has to be straightforward; "local company triples its production while cutting its expenses in half - without layoffs".  It has to be very simple, very straight and it has to be something newsworthy. That example was just off the top of my head, but that will get somebody's attention. You can't make them guess. If they have to guess what it's about, there's a real good chance they hit the delete button instead.

**MR:** It's almost like developing a benefit driven USP (unique selling proposition, something that sets you apart from the pack).

**BW:** It is. It's exactly a benefit-driven USP but it's for the benefit of that journalist. What you really have to do. What you really have to do is you practically do the whole job for them. They're overworked, understaffed, underappreciated, underloved. What you have to do is pretty well offer to do the whole job for them. It's kind of like PLR. You're almost like doing PLR writing. You're doing the whole thing and you're going to let them put their name on it.

**MR:** That's awesome. Well. Honestly, I'm not one to hype people up. I'm not one to be like these other people "we need to make more sales." Let me let you all know I'm not trying to dip in to Brother Brian's pocket. that $97. That's his friend-of-a-friend discounted rate. That's all his money. I'm not getting affiliate commission for that. I've known Brother Brian for a number of years. Brother Brian has been an action taker. Brother Brian has implemented stuff that I've told him to do and he's actually been able to make a living off of some of the training that I've shared with him like on membership sites way back in the day, the early days of Internet marketing coaching club and stuff. I know Brother Brian. He is legit, there's a lot more about this man that you guys don't know. So to be able to book an hour of his time for just $97, that's a freaking steal.  It is honestly a steal because this is a professional that you guys are basically "hiring" to spend time with you and to help you, laser target and hone in your marketing message, make it more news worthy to try to get you to establish that rapport, that relationship with these news contacts so that the next time you guys got something like a word out there about, you are ready to go. Not only is he providing you the tools. But he's willing to extend his time. $97 ain't nothing Brother Brian. I mean, I actually dad you work with my wife and I know how serious you are and how - what's the word I'm looking for...

**BW:** Intense?

**MR:** Not only intense but complete... You're really, really thorough.

**BW:** Thorough. Yes.

**MR:** Very thorough. Listen. take advantage of it. brother Brian, are you going to limit how many people you're going to do? or are you just going to say "Hey! first come first serve and when I get tired of doing that offer, I'll stop offering"?

**BW:** You know what. If they are your friends, I'll make sure I'll fit them in somehow, but obviously I don't know how long I'm going to be able to keep the rate that low. But let me just point out something because people who haven't doe these before might not get it. If you get a professional journalist/writer/anchorman to take your idea, put it to a press release that will be picked up, the going rate for that is $200. If you then have them put it out across one of the real prestige authority outlets like Vocus or PR Web, that's another $150-$200. So I'm going to show you how to do all that in one hour.

**MR:** Dang Brother Brian. that is sick. I'm going to, probably, pick that up for myself as well even thought I got like crazy access to you because we'll be talking about a lot of stuff in Native American spirituality; we've been talking about politics. we'll be talking about your knighthood. If you guys get that hour with Brother Brian, make sure you ask him the question because he's an actual knight. he's been knighted. I'm not going to tell you by which royal family. You're going to hear that once you hook up with him.

**BW:** I can update you, man. I've got six knighthoods and two baronies.

**MR:** That is sick, man. I can't stand you no more! You keep growing up in that royalty. Not only are you Native American royalty, you're growing up in all these other countries being knighted and becoming a baron. but let me ask you. I've got to sweeten the pot and make the deal a little better. I want to ask you a personal favor. For those people that do the $97 personal one hour time with you to do what they got to do to get that either confidence or to get that professionalism or to get that news stories subject line, whatever it is they're going to work with you for that hour, would you mind doing me a favor for these folks and can you record that one hour session do it via Skype. would you mind recording it for them and then giving them a copy of the recording so that they could have? So they are not practically writing notes. So they can always go back and listen to what you said.

**BW:** Sure, I could throw that in.

**MR:** Brother Brian is like "Dangit. You're making me do more work." I mean, I'm just saying, if it was me, I would want to record my one hour session with you and if you're able to do that for them as an added bonus, that's an unannounced bonus like "Look, you hire me for an hour, not only will I give you my hour of my time. I'm going to record it and then give you and mp3 recording of it so that you can always go back and listen to it for yourself." They know they are not going to share that stuff. it's just one-on-one for them.

**BW:** It's not to be cut up for an audio product or PLR audio or anything. That is just because they'll be talking about their business that will be confidential. everything will be in confidence for my end. I presume it will be from their end as well.

**MR:** I got to ask you one more thing brother Brian. Are you willing, as something totally separate... this isn't part of the bonus, but I remember outsourcing my students and clients to you for voice over work? Are you still open and willing to doing voice over work?

**BW:** Sure. I can still do that. I mean, I'm *doing* that, I'm just doing it on my own products.

**MR:** And you've been doing commercials for the city and the radio and stuff like that. For those of you that are interested in that as well, Brother Brian, you guys can hire him to do voiceover work, and let me tell you, the rate that he was giving my students and clients in the past, is sick, ridiculous cheap. So when you guys are ready, you want Brother Brian to do a voice over for you, maybe even pitch that story for you in that booming voice.

How many of you guys know somebody like that? You could go on and say "man. I've got this awesome voice over talent who's got years of professional experience, tons of knowledge and he's willing to impart on me." You guys can book him for an hour for $97 and if you decided to take a step further, you can always hire Brother Brian to do your voice over work and stuff like that. But trust me. Going with Brother Brian, you cannot go wrong. He's going to help you get your news story out there. He's going to help you establish as an instant expert and authority in Internet marketer niche. you cannot go wrong with Brother Brian. He's very ethical, very professional. He's a spiritual brother. he's prayed for me and my family. He's been there for me in so many more ways that I can never thank him enough. thank you so much for this time with you Brother Brian. God bless you. I'm going to let you have the last parting words.

**BW:** Well. then, the last parting words are God bless you Mark. God bless your wonderful family, and I had my head spun around about a week or so listening to a recording that you did on a radio show in somewhere there in Southern California. I say somewhere because I haven't been out there. I don't know where things are but I listen to your little daughter explaining something that really everybody should learn. Do you want to quote that?

**MR:** I said I let you have the parting words but it's awesome. Thank you for bringing that up. when I did that radio show, they actually interviewed my entire family. that's the influence that came with that particular topic and subject matter. they interviewed my mother, my wife, my daughter and myself. My daughter is a 7 year old. What my daughter said was "when you guys start to feel this negative and insecurity and all these stuff, you guys feel like you can't do something, you're just not confident," she said "press pause on your negative thoughts and press play on your positive thoughts." That's coming from my 7-year-old daughter. The radio host was just floored with her. She's like "God! at 7 years old", that was from Sabrina. So thank you for bringing that up Brother Brian. God bless you. We'll talk to you soon. And everybody that's listening to this, thank you so much for your time as well. we appreciate and value you for listening to this as well. Buh-bye!

# About the Author

**Brian Wilkes** has been involved in every area of journalism. Although originally a political cartoonist, he also did radio newscasts starting in 1972, and had a brief interview with one of the Watergate burglars during the lead-up to the Congressional hearings. He has been anchor and talk show host for **WILO** in Frankfort, IN, news director of NBC affiliate **WRKT-WMOD** in Cocoa, Florida, and of CBS affiliate **WMEL** in Melbourne, Florida, where he made his reputation for coverage of the space program.

Wilkes was part of the team hired to transition West Palm Beach music station **WJNO** to an news-talk format in 1979, where we was news anchor, medical editor, features editor, drama and film critic, covering world leaders and international celebrities. In 1984, he set up a training program for volunteer journalists at **WBAI-FM** in New York. His work has received many awards for new coverage, documentary production, and commentary. He has also worked in newspaper, wire service, magazine and television media.

In 1985, he was recommended for spaceflight by a Apollo astronaut Al Worden and the nation's first TV news director. Spencer Allen of **WGN-TV** in Chicago. Even though NASA's "Journalist In Space" project was shelved after the Challenger explosion in January, 1986, he regards the recommendation as one of the highest honors of his career.

Quick to see the implications of Internet as a new medium, he launched Brian Wilkes Media (now Tuscany Global Corporation) in 2000, which creates and delivers educational programs and publications worldwide. His firm provides consulting, coaching and training to small businesses, and originated the **"SHOCK and AWE"** promotional system he uses to put clients on Page 1 of Google in as little as an hour.

Wilkes also teaches photography, and serves a select international clientele in hypnotherapy, neuro-linguistic programming, Usui Reiki, Qigong, and traditional Native American healing.

*Other Titles from Tuscany Global:*

Please view and download our current Catalog!

**http://tuscanyglobal.com/catalog/**

For the consulting special Mark Ress mentioned, please contact **BWilkes@TuscanyGlobal.com**

*Tuscany*
GLOBAL CORPORATION